*The Knowledge of God
in Mechthild of
Magdeburg*

The Knowledge of God in Mechthild of Magdeburg

Christina Manohar

Tercentenary Publication
2010

The Knowledge of God in Mechthild of Magdeburg - Published by the Rev. Dr. Ashish Amos of the Indian Society for Promoting Christian Knowledge (ISPCK), Post Box 1585, 1654, Madarsa Road, Kashmere Gate, Delhi-110006 under its Women's Empowerment Programme (WEP-19).

© Author, 2010

ISBN: 978-81-8465-070-9

Laser typeset at **ISPCK,** Post Box 1585, 1654, Madarsa Road, Kashmere Gate, Delhi-110006

Tel: 23866323, 23866322

e-mail–ashish@ispck.org.in • ella@ispck.org.in

website-www.ispck.org.in

Dedicated
to
My Mother
with
Love and Gratitude

Contents

Foreword

Mysticism is an aspect of religion in which many faiths tend to converge, and we can see many similarities and parallels in the experiences and writings of mystics of diverse provenance. For instance scholars have drawn attention to the striking similarities in the conceptual thinking and imagery of St John of the Cross and the famous Sufi mystic, Jalal al Din al Rumi.

Looking at the writings of Mechthild of Magdeburg and the divine- human relationship that she reveals in her writings one is struck by how similar it is to the thoughts and experience of the Muslim Rabia al Adawiya or of the Hindu Mirabai. Accounts of mystical experience are therefore fascinating to all scholars of religion, whatever faith group their chosen field of study, and also to the wider readership who have an interest in the mystery of religious experience.

This study and appraisal of Mechthild's writings by Dr Christina Manohar is a very lucid, beautifully written exposition and analysis. Dr Manohar has explored widely and her analysis has benefited from many sources both old and new which give this study much authenticity and value. Moreover the discussion touches upon a variety of highly interesting aspects of a woman mystic's life, the nature of the visions, the obvious sexual connotations implied in the narratives of this passionate encounter of the human and the divine, the agony and the ecstasy of these religious experiences. The comparative element is also introduced with references to Hildegard of Bingen and Julian of Norwich and even male mystics such as Bernard of Clairvaux.

Important also is the theme of suffering and how God's love is reflected not only in the euphoria and even ecstasy of these divine-human encounters but also the way in which God subjects those whom he loves to trials and suffering. The analysis also considers the issue of feminism, particularly the experience of women mystics at the hands of male clerical hierarchy, and the boldness with which Mechthild withstands criticism and opposition drawing strength from her relationship with God.

On the whole this is indeed a valuable study with useful insights into the amazing religious experience of a Christian woman mystic in the medieval context of religious obscurantism and chauvinism. This book is of benefit not only to Christian theologians but also to all scholars of religion.

Theodore Gabriel
Dr. Theodore Gabriel
Associate Senior Lecturer and Honorary Research Fellow
(Theology and Religious Studies)
Department of Humanities
University of Gloucestershire

Preface

Mechthild of Magdeburg, a medieval woman mystic who saw herself as an instrument of divine will, wrote and established her spiritual authority in the midst of interconnected struggles of power and gender. The primary concern of this work is Mechthild's knowledge of God. Many writers such as Frank Tobin, Barbara Newman, Sarah Poor, Caroline Walker Bynum and others have written a great deal on Mechthild's life and writings. However, the theme, the knowledge of God, has not been elaborated sufficiently. Hence this work seeks to highlight woman's ways of being, knowing and doing. Mechthild's own highest spiritual experiences come from her inner depths. The knowledge of God occurs in the intimate loving relationship between the soul and God. Vision is a mode of perception. Divine depth dimension is perceived in visions, experienced, appropriated and re-presented to the readers and thus Mechthild's experience and knowledge of God is re-created in the readers and even brings new knowledge to them. Her book *The Flowing Light of Divinity* has much to say about the divine-human immediacy in charming courtly language. This study shows that her knowledge is an embodied knowledge since it integrates feeling, passion and physical/biological knowing that does not negate intellect and that can be situated in the affective tradition of the medieval age yet with a difference. The independence that is shown in her writings and the mixing of emotional and intellectual elements reveal her as a mystic of her own kind. Her writings call for an epistemological modesty formed in the recognition that male judgement and voices need to be tested by listening to other voices that are previously excluded or ignored. They also call for an epistemological privilege for women's voice since their voices and woman's way of knowing were not taken into serious consideration and still are not heard as they should be heard.

This study was undertaken when I was going through a very difficult time in life. Each day as I sat in the library of the University of Gloucestershire, reflecting upon the ways of knowing God, Mechthild's life and teachings reminded me once more that one needs to discover the continuing presence of the light in the midst of darkness. May this study offer every reader a thirst for the intimate, loving relationship with the living God. May the flowing light of divinity kindle each heart and radiate light into the darkness.

Christina Manohar
Cheltenham
2009

Introduction

echthild, a captivating medieval woman writer was born around 1207 in Saxony, Magdeburg. Her family belonged to a knightly class. From early on she was well acquainted with courtly culture, urban life and the preaching of mendicant orders, Franciscans and Dominicans, whom she regarded highly.[1] At the age of twelve she had the extraordinary spiritual experience of being greeted by the Holy Spirit. This was a great and overwhelming experience that turned her into an intensely spiritual person. She had several visions and began to experience God more intensely.[2]

Around 1230, probably in her early twenties, she joined the house of Beguines in Magdeburg.[3] She followed the

---

[1] Mechthild von Magdeburg, *The Flowing Light of Divinity*, translated by Christiane Mesch Galvani, edited with introduction by Susan Clark, Series B: Garland Library of Medieval Literature, 72 (New York & London: Garland Publishing, 1991), Book 5.24, pp. 152-54.

[2] Book 4.2; Galvani, pp. 95-100, p. 96. Hildegard of Bingen also claims that she had visionary experiences from her childhood. She claimed that both vision and meaning were imprinted on her memory. See Rosemary Radford Reuther, *Visionary Women: Three Medieval Mystics* (Minneapolis: Fortress Press, 2002), pp. 30-31, p. 7.

[3] For more details, see Sara S. Poor, "Mechthild von Magdeburg, Gender, and the 'Unlearned Tongue'", *Journal of Medieval and Early Modern Studies*, 31, no. 2 (2001), 213-250, p. 217ff.

Beguines' way of life for about forty years and she may have served as its head at some point. Beguines were laywomen who lived in small communities or together in houses and earned their living by engaging themselves in small cottage industries such as weaving and other handwork. They even lived by begging. They led a life of poverty, chastity, ascetical practices and prayer. Like Franciscans, they wore a uniform dress of gray. They took vows of chastity but this did not prevent them from marrying. Although, they lived a life of piety and engaged in social work such as nursing the sick and teaching, they were not governed by any ecclesial authorities or bound by any monastic rules.[4] Later on, in 1223 the Beguines received quasi-legal recognition from Pope Gregory IX and were under clerical authorities. However, this did not take away their freedom and they were never seen as an official religious order.[5] "The more developed beguinage was like a small religious settlement in the midst of a city. Entrance to the closed circle of cottages, which served as residences for the Beguines, would be through one main gate, and often a surrounding wall or a canal would offer further security and identity. A beguinage would also include a church, as well as buildings for community work, dispensing charity and administration."[6]

---

[4] Rosemary Radford Ruether, *Visionary Women: Three Medieval Mystics,* pp.30-31. Also ref. to Sarah S. Poor, "Historicizing Canonicity: Tradition and the Invisible Talent of Mechthild von Magdeburg", *Women in German Year Book* 15 (2000), pp. 49-72, note 11 on p. 67. Charlotte Allen, "The Holy Feminine", *First Things,* 98 (1999), 37-44, p. 43. For the socio-economic aspects of beguine movement see, Walter Simons, *Cities of Ladies: Beguine Communities in the Medieval Low Countries, 1200- 1565* (Philadelphia: University of Pennsylvania Press, 2001).

[5] Roger Schroeder, SVD, "Women, Mission and the Early Franciscan Movement", *Missiology,* 28, no. 4 (2000), 411-424, p. 416.

[6] *Ibid.*

Often Beguines were treated suspiciously by others. They were considered as heretics. Many times, Mechthild had to defend herself against such accusations since the male clergies were not convinced by her claims of visionary authority.[7] Although Mechthild was certain of her visionary authority, unfortunately she lacked the support of the church to defend and protect her from criticisms since such claim by a woman was considered audacious in the thirteenth century. Women in general were often ignored by the church and literary establishment, which were controlled by the male interpreters.[8]

Perhaps because of such struggles and conflicts or, perhaps, because of the poor health she suffered, Mechthild left the Beguine community and lived with her relatives for some time. She then entered the Cistercian convent at Helfta in around the year 1270.[9] Helfta was a centre of literary activity, the religious community at Helfta was a place where medieval women writers such as Gertrude the Great (ca.1256-1302) and Mechthild of Hackeborn (1241- 1299) were nurtured and in this convent Mechthild of Magdeburg spent her last years. She probably died around 1282.[10]

Unlike the Beguine community, the Cistercian convent was financially secure and was under ecclesiastical authority. Another difference between Beguine community and the convent at Helfta is that a structured education of theology was available at the Helfta convent. It was a seat of learning

---

[7] Books 2.24, 4.2, 9.11 and 7.28; Galvani, pp. 49-52, p. 50; pp. 95-100, p. 96; pp. 138-139, p. 138 and pp. 195-96, p. 195.

[8] Frank Tobin, *Mechthild von Magdeburg: A Medieval Mystic in Modern Eyes* (Columbia: Camden House, 1995), p. 125.

[9] *Ibid.,* p. 2.

[10] Susan Clark, "Introduction", *Flowing Light of Divinity*, pp. xiv-xv.

and piety. The sisters in the convent were well educated and looked up to Mechthild as an object of veneration and looked for instruction from her. Mechthild felt that she was unlearned and ignorant in this environment. But always her focus had been the heart. Mechthild did not have any academic education. Sex and class often determined opportunities to education in the medieval age. Only a few had the opportunity to learn and to acquire education that gave access to "the medium that equated power: the word, and, by extension, the Word."[11]

Most probably, Mechthild would have received instructions in all facets of spirituality from the priest who attended the community's needs during her stay in the Beguine community. Obviously, she did not have formal education in a convent and received no learning in Latin. Lack of knowledge of Latin would have deprived her to access the western religious tradition.[12] Hence, when she was asked to teach by the Helfta nuns, Mechthild felt that she was ignorant and unlearned. She tells them, "you ask me to teach you, when I myself am ignorant. You will find a thousandfold in your books what you desire..."[13] However, Mechthild did engage in writing. She was one of the few women, who could write and did write and whose works were preserved although we are not certain how much of her works were preserved.[14] She claimed that she received a command from God to write down her spiritual experiences. She began writing her spiritual

---

[11] *Ibid.*, pp. xv-xvi.

[12] Frank Tobin, *Mechthild von Magdeburg: A Medieval Mystic in Modern Eyes*, p. 71.

[13] Book 7:21; Galvani, pp. 226-227, p. 226.

[14] See, Susan Clark, "Introduction", *Flowing Light of Divinity*, p. xi.

experiences about 1250 and completed them in Helfta, dictating the last chapters due to her failing eyesight.[15]

Mechthild, in her autobiographical writings aims to show her stages of spiritual life. They were written with the intention of instructing and spiritually edifying the readers. Mechthild thought that she was the chosen instrument of God and she felt compelled within her to write. Wolfgang Mohr rightly comments, "She sees it, rather, as a recording of immediate experiences over which she has no control. If she does compare herself with other writers, it is with the prophets or the inspired writers of the Bible, who are reduced to instruments of the divine will, that she feels affinity."[16]

Mechthild probably noted down her mystical revelations in a "loose leaf format" or dictated at random her insights into both divine and secular matters over a number of years. These were later on collected and copied by the Dominican Heinrich of Halle. Heinrich was probably her spiritual advisor or father confessor. Mechthild confided her spiritual experiences to him. These collections were then taken by a sect called 'Friends of God'[17] which duly translated her low

---

[15] Frank Tobin, *Mechthild von Magdeburg: A Medieval Mystic in Modern Eyes*, pp. 2-3.

[16] Wolfgang Mohr, "Darbietungsformen der Mystik bei Mechthild von Magdeburg", in *Märchen, Mythos, Dichtung: Festschrift zum 90*, Geburtstag Friedrich von der Leyens, ed. Hugo Kuhn and Kurt Schier, Munich Beck, 1963, pp. 375-99, p. 377, cited in Frank Tobin, *Mechthild von Magdeburg: A Medieval Mystic in Modern Eyes*, p. 75.

[17] The Friends of God was a group of both religious and lay people, which was active in Basel, Strasberg, and Köln during the fourteenth century. They focused on intimate relationship with God and revered the writings of religious men and women. Patricia Zimmerman Beckman, "The Power of Books and the Practice of Mysticism in the Fourteenth Century: Heinrich Nördlingen and Margaret Ebner on Mechthild's Flowing Light of the Godhead", *Church History*, 76, no. 1(2007), 61-83, p. 73.

German dialect into Alemmanic in order to make it available to those who could not understand her low German dialect.[18]

Mechthild calls her book *Das fleßendes Licht der Gottheit* (*The Flowing Light of the Divinity* or *A Flowing Light of My Divinity*) since the living Divinity flowed forth into her heart[19] and she wished to honour only God by her writing. She writes,

> 'O, Lord, who has made this book? I, in my own incompetence have made it because I cannot keep my gift to myself. Oh, Lord, how shall this book be called? To honor only You? It shall be called: *A Flowing Light of My Divinity*, flowing into the hearts of all those who live without falsehood.'[20]

Books One to Six of *The Flowing Light of the Divinity* are generally held to have been composed at Magdeburg and Book Seven, was probably written at Helfta during her last years. However, as mentioned above, her writings reveal that the male clergy and ecclesiastical hierarchy did not appreciate her for her writings. For instance, Books 2.26; 3.5; 6.38, show that she was warned against writing. In Book 2.26, she says,

---

[18] See, Susan Clark, "Introduction", *Flowing Light of Divinity*, p. xii. Reuther gives some information of Mechthild's original writing and the translation and edition done by others."The Low German original of Mechthild's book has not been found. Around 1290 Heinrich of Halle, who collected and organized the original Low German version, translated it into Latin as *Lux Divinitatis fluens in corda veritatis*. This version, on parchment, is in the university library of Basel. About 1344-45, Henrich of Nördlingen and the Friends of God in Basel made a translation of the Low German text into Middle High German, the only copy of which is in the library of the Benedictine Monastery of Einsiedeln. This text, plus a free translation into modern German, was published by Morel Gall in 1869. The best modern version of the fourteenth-century text is edited by Hans Neumann, published in 1990." Rosemary Radford Ruether, *Visionary Women: Three Medieval Mystics*, note 61, on p. 70.

[19] Book 6.43; Galvani, p. 206.

[20] Book 1; Galvani, p. 5.

> I was warned about this book and was told by men
> That it should not be preserved
> But destroyed by fire.
> Then I did what I have done since childhood,
> And that is to pray when I am troubled.
> I leaned toward my loved one and said:
> 'Alas, Lord, now I am very troubled.
> For Your glory I must remain unconsoled away from You.
> You have misled me
> In making me write this book.'
> At that God immediately revealed Himself
> To my sad soul, holding this book in His right hand,
> And said: 'My love, do not upset yourself too much;
> The truth cannot be burned by anyone.
> He who wants to take it from My hand
> Must be stronger than I.'[21]

Mechthild tells God,

> 'Alas, Lord, were I a learned man
> And You had worked this miracle in me
> It would forever bring You glory.
> But how can anyone believe
> That You have built a golden house
> In this filthy slough',[22]

The Lord replies

> 'I always sought for the lowest,
> The least, the best concealed place.
> The highest mountain cannot receive

---

[21] Book 2.26; Galvani, pp. 55-58, pp. 55-56.
[22] Book 2.26; Galvani, pp. 55-58, p. s56.

> The revelation of My grace,
>
> For the flood of My Holy Spirit
>
> Flows by nature into the valley.'[23]

She records a vision in which "God identifies her book with God's Trinitarian nature: the parchment on which it was written as God's humanity, the words that flew into her soul as God's divinity, and the voice of these words as the Holy Spirit."[24] She writes,

> This book came from God.
>
> 'I do not speak from my senses.
>
> It is love which makes me speak.'[25]

Thus, Mechthild claims that this book itself has come from "Love's industry."[26] In fact, Mechthild thinks that the whole purpose of God creating humanity is to befriend them, love them and in turn be loved by them. God's intense desire is to love and to be loved. She writes in book 3.9 where the Trinity in conversation expresses the desire to create humanity to love.

> Then the Eternal Son said with great politeness: 'Dear Father, my nature, too, should bear fruit...Let Us pattern mankind after Me, although I foresee great sorrow since I must love man eternally.' The Father replied, 'Son, I, too, am moved by a powerful desire in my breast, and I hear the sound of love. We shall become fruitful in order to be loved in return...I will create Bride for Myself who shall greet Me with her mouth and wound Me with her look; only then will love begin.' And the Holy Spirit said to the Father: 'Yes, dear father, I will bring the Bride to Your

---

[23] Book 2.26; Galvani, pp. 55-58, pp. 56-57.

[24] Rosemary Radford Ruether, *Visionary Women: Three Medieval Mystics*, p. 32, citing Book 2.26.

[25] Book 4.2; Galvani, pp. 95-100, p. 99.

[26] Book 6.20; Galvani, pp. 190-91.

bed.' ...Then the Holy Trinity leaned over the creation of all things and created us, body and soul, with untold love.

Her theological anthropology is based on this Trinitarian vision and she has much to say about the soul's relationship with God the Beloved and it is in this relationship that the knowledge of God occurs.

Part - I

The Knowledge of God
in
Mechthild of Magdeburg (ca. 1207-83)

Knowing God in the Intimate Relationship

The soul's relationship to God is the essential feature of Mechthild's writings. It is expressed in most charming images. The soul longs for God. No creature can fully imagine the soul's longing for God.[1] Much of her theology comes through poetry. Mechthild often uses courtly language.[2] For instance, in books 1 and 2 Mechthild uses adjectives from the courtly sphere. Her writings reveal that she was familiar with the court. She may well have enjoyed a courtly upbringing and was therefore familiar with the courtly lyric poetry of the previous generations. Perhaps her refined writing and courtly images are "based on remembrances of personal experiences."[3]

Love that occurs in the secular courtly poem receives a spiritual meaning in Mechthild's writings. As Frank Tobin observes, "the idea of nobility, noble titles and places, the courtly feast and lyric poetry, and courtly code of ethics" are expressed in her poems. However, she does include images from the Bible, particularly from the Song of Songs.[4] She speaks

---

[1] Book 5. 31; Galvani, pp. 160-161.

[2] For courtly language see also Book 1.14; Galvani, p. 12.

[3] Frank Tobin, *Mechthild von Magdeburg: A Medieval Mystic in Modern Eyes*, p. 1.

[4] *Ibid.*, p. 41.

of a soul as a noble maiden, Christ as a handsome youth. The lady soul waits for the youth, the beloved God, and longs to dance with him. Love is the way to union with the beloved[5] and the soul cannot exist without God. The soul says to God,

'O God, You abound with Your gifts!

You flow with love!

You burn with desire!

You melt in the union with Your love!

You rest on my breasts, and I cannot exist without You!'[6]

God descends on the soul and enters the soul "as the dew on the flowers."[7] The soul is imbued with God and enveloped. The Lord penetrates the soul, says to the soul,

'You are My yearning, a loving wish;

You are a sweet refreshment to My breast,

You are a powerful kiss to My mouth,

You are the gleeful joy of My revelation;

I am in you and you are in Me.

We could not be closer

For we are fused together,

Poured into one mould,

And so we shall remain forever undaunted.'[8]

Phrases such as 'God entering the soul', 'penetrating the soul' and the soul being enveloped by God, inform the reader how Mechthild experienced God in an intimate personal way.

---

[5] See Book I.44; Galvani, pp. 22-26, p. 26; Book 4.1; Galvani, p. 95.
[6] Book 1.17; Galvani, p. 13.
[7] Book 1.13; Galvani, p. 12.
[8] Book 3.5; Galvani, pp. 70-71.

Further, God says to the soul "I am in you and you are in Me"[9]; the soul and the Beloved are "fused together and poured into one mould."[10] This suggests divine-human immediacy.

This divine-human immediacy is expressed in many ways in Mechthild's writings. The soul and God gaze at each other lovingly. It is a blessed exchange; for worldly pleasures and riches, heavenly freedom and God Himself with all His riches are granted to the soul.[11] "The gaze between God and the loving soul, which passes between them so blissfully, has such strength and glow"[12] that the soul knows her Beloved in this sweet exchange of gaze. The soul says that she who is the companion of God's love, has no love of her own for she is forever moved by God.[13] All things are beautiful between the soul and the loving God.[14] God says to the soul "I am the light and your breast is the lantern."[15] They embrace each other, kiss, they reluctantly part from each other. She is enveloped, enjoys the nuptial pleasure. She mingles in the Holy Trinity yet remains in herself.[16] The only prayer of the soul is to ask God to love her more deeply that she may become purer, holier and more beautiful:

> 'Ah, Lord, love me much, and love me deeply and for a long time; for the more deeply you love me, the purer I shall become; the more you love me, the more beautiful I shall become; the longer you love me, the holier I shall become here on earth.'[17]

---

[9] Book 3.5; Galvani, pp. 70-71, p. 70.

[10] *Ibid.*

[11] Book 1.1; Galvani, pp. 5-6.

[12] Book 5.1; Galvani, pp. 129-130.

[13] Book 1.44; Galvani, pp. 22-26, p. 23.

[14] Book 3.11; Galvani, p. 78.

[15] Book 3.12; Galvani, pp. 78-79.

[16] Book 1.22; Galvani, pp. 14-16, pp. 14-15.

[17] Book 1.23; Galvani, p. 16.

God does not disappoint the soul for God is love and loving is his nature. God answers the soul saying, "Loving you ardently is my nature, for I myself am love, loving you much from My longing, for I long to be loved much in return. Loving you for a long time comes from My eternity, for I am infinite."[18] Loving God draws the soul to Himself. It is a rare elevated path; the soul by submitting herself to God treads towards her lover.

In Book 1.29, God assumes himself as bridegroom and addresses the soul as his bride or wife. God the husband draws the attention of his wife by speaking these words: "See, my wife: see how beautiful My eyes are, how right My mouth is, how fiery My heart is, how agile My hands are, how quick My feet are, and follow Me. ..."[19] God likens the soul to a beautiful rose among the thorns, flying bee in the honey, pure dove, beautiful sun and full moon.[20] God says that he cannot turn from the soul and he caresses her saying, 'You are My pillow, My lovely bed, My secret resting place, My deepest desire, My highest honor. You are joy in My Divinity, solace to My Humanity, a cooling brook to My fervor.'[21]

In a lovely embrace the soul and the beloved God become one like water and wine. The knowledge of God takes place or occurs in this embrace as she is consumed by Him. The soul becomes the reflection of God.

> The poor soul is well-spoken and well-behaved when she comes to court, and she cheerfully looks at her God. Ah, how lovingly she is received. She is silent and longingly awaits His praise. He reveals His divine heart to her with great eagerness. It is like the golden red flame of burning coals. He takes her into His glowing heart, just as the noble prince and the little servant-girl embrace and become one like water

---

18 Book 1.24; Galvani, p. 16.
19 Book 1.29; Galvani, p. 18.
20 Book 1.18; Galvani, p. 13.
21 Book 1.19; Galvani, p. 13.

and wine. She is consumed by Him and takes leave of herself; when she has had enough, He is more lovesick for her than He ever was before when He desired more. She says: 'Lord, You are my comfort, my desire, my flowing well, my sun, and I am Your reflection. ' This is a visit to the court which, without God, would not have been possible.[22]

Thus, Mechthild's emotional and affective aspects of love are expressed through the traditions of bride mysticism. Mechthild explains spiritual marriage as "fusion of her nature with the divine nature" or "becoming one mould"[23] so that the Lord can say to the 'Lady Soul' "I am in you and you are in Me."[24] "You are so much a part of My nature that nothing can be between you and Me."[25] Although there is a fusion, a kind of oneness as water and wine become one, yet Mechthild's dialogue with God suggests it is not an absorption but a transformation into divine nature. The distinction between the soul and the Beloved are still maintained in the oneness.[26] The soul praises God and God in turn praises the soul. The soul recognises the presence of God and praises God and God recognises the presence of the other, the soul and praises her. The soul says,

---

[22] Book 1.4; Galvani, p. 9.

[23] Book 3.5; Galvani, pp. 70-71, p. 70.

[24] *Ibid.*

[25] Book 1. 44; Galvani, pp. 22-26, p. 25.

[26] The image of mixed liquids was used not only by Mechthild but by many other writers including Bernard of Clairvaux who like Mechthild never advocated a kind of oneness or loss of distinctiveness between the soul and the Lord. But later on, this image was associated with the 'Free Spirit heresy'; a heresy which mixed gnostic beliefs with Christian tenets of faith. The followers of 'Free Spirit heresy' believed that perfection can be attained in this world through a life of austerity and spiritualism. Their interpretation of the image of mixed liquids blurred the distinctiveness between the subject and object. For this reason, this image was held with apprehension by some in the late medieval age. See, Robert E. Lerner, "The Image of Mixed Liquids in Late Medieval Mystical Thought", *Church History*, 40, no.4 (1971), pp. 397-411.

'O, sweet Jesus, most beautiful form unconcealed in distress and love in the wretched soul, I praise You in love, in need, in joy, in fellowship alike with all other creatures. I desire that above all other things, Lord, You are the sun of all eyes, the pleasure of all ears, You are the voice of all words, You are the strength of all goodness, You are the teacher of all wisdom, the love of all life, the order of all being. Then God praised the loving soul in which He took delight: 'You are the light of My eyes, the lyre of My ears, the voice of My words, the purpose of My goodness, the honor of My wisdom; a love in My life, you are a praise of My being.'[27]

God says to the soul,

'You are a light to the world!

You are a crown to maidens

You are balsam to the wounded

You are loyalty to the false

You are a bride of the Holy Trinity.'[28]

In the following dialogue between the soul and the Beloved the oneness is maintained but not without distinction between the two.

'When I shine, you must glow.

When I flow, you must rage,

When you sigh, you draw My divine heart to you;

When you weep near Me, I take you into My arms.

But when you love Me, the two of us become one,

And when that happens, no one can come between us.

Instead, a blissful hesitation will dwell between the two of us.

---

27 Book 3.2; Galvani, pp. 66-67.
28 Book 2.9; Galvani, p. 39.

Lord, so I shall wait hungrily and thirstily,

Breathlessly and eagerly,

Until that playful hour

When from Your divine mouth

Will flow the chosen words

Which will be heard by no one

But that soul alone,

Who removes the earth from herself

And lends her ears to Your mouth

Indeed, she comprehends love's treasure trove.'[29]

In Mechthild's presentation of dialogue between the soul and the beloved, the human and divine voices are joined like image and reflection. The soul says, "You are my highest mirror image, a feast for my eyes, the loss of my self, the storm in my heart, the downfall and failure of my power, my highest expectation."[30] In Book 3.11, God is spoken of as an eternal mirror and the loving soul gazes into the eternal mirror.

In the dialogues between the soul and God, it becomes clear that heart[31] is the place of God. The soul says, "You, Lord, are my treasure, You are also my heart, and You alone are my good, ..."[32] God asks the soul what she is bringing: "you are very rushed in love; tell me, what do you bring Me, My queen?"[33] She replies "Lord, I bring you my gem: it is taller than the mountains, wider than the world, deeper than the sea, Higher than the clouds, fairer than the sun, more multitudinous than

---

[29] Book 2.6; Galvani, p. 37.

[30] Book 1.20; Galvani, p. 13.

[31] Book 1.39-43; Galvani, p. 21.

[32] Book 4.7; Galvani, p. 106.

[33] Book 1.39; Galvani, p. 21.

the stars, weightier than all the earth."[34] Praising her, God asks the Name of the Gem, "Your image of My Divinity, ennobled by My Humanity, adorned with My Holy Spirit, what is the name of your gem?"[35] She replies that the gem is called the pleasure of the heart, "Lord, it is called the pleasure of my heart, which I have removed from the world, retained for myself, and denied to all creatures; now I can carry it no further. Lord, where shall I place it?"[36] God asks her to place her pleasure in the Holy Trinity: "You shall place the pleasure of your heart nowhere but in My divine heart and at My human breast. There alone will you be comforted and kissed by My spirit."[37]

When speaking about the intimacy between God and the soul, Mechthild makes it clear that God for her is the Trinity. The soul praises the Trinity.[38] In the closest proximity, the soul understands, knows and praises God. Such knowledge that comes by way of the intimate relationship with God can be stated as knowing God with one's soul's eyes or seeing God with one's soul's eyes.

---

[34] Book 1.40; Galvani, p. 21.

[35] Book 1.41; Galvani, p. 21.

[36] Book 1.42; Galvani, p. 21.

[37] Book 1.43; Galvani, p. 21.

[38] Book 5.6; Galvani, p. 135.

Knowing God with the Eyes of the Soul

Mechthild claims that her knowledge of God comes by seeing God with the eyes of her soul. She says, "I do not know how nor can I write unless I see it with the eyes of my soul and hear it with the ears of my eternal spirit..."[1] Similarly, another medieval writer, Hildegard of Bingen (1098-1179) called her way of knowing God as knowing through "the eyes of the spirit and the inner ear."[2] Jerome Gellman explains that "it is knowledge that is available through non-sensory means but it does not mean that sensory content is absent."[3] Mechthild says about the writing of her book: "The writing of this book is seen, heard, and felt in all limbs – 'I cannot nor do I wish to write, except that I see it with my eyes and my soul, and I hear it with the ears of my eternal spirit and feel it in all the members of my body: the power of the Holy Spirit.'"[4] Perhaps what Mechthild and Hildegard are speaking about is an extraordinary sensory input occurring along with the knowledge that is available through sensory or non-sensory means.

---

[1] Book 4.13; Galvani, p. 119.

[2] See, Jerome Gellman, *Mystical Experience of God: A Philosophical Inquiry* (England: Ashgate Publishing Limited, 2001), p. 5.

[3] *Ibid.*

[4] Book 4.13; Galvani, p. 111.

In the following poem, it becomes clear that Mechthild's knowledge of God comes by seeing God with the enlightened eyes of her soul. The knowledge of God stems from intimacy between her and God. All through her writing, as stated earlier, Mechthild speaks about the intimacy between the soul and God in many ways. Here, the intimacy is like God clothing himself with the soul. God is her closest dress. God shines into her soul. This is the source of her knowledge of her beloved.

The Lord clothes himself with the soul. The soul declares,

'You shine into my soul

As the sun onto gold.

When I must repose in You, Lord,

My joy is multifold.

You clothe Yourself with my soul,

And You, in turn, are her closest dress.

The thought of parting from You

Causes me the greatest of heartaches.

If You were to love me more,

I would surely pass away,

For it is my wish

To love You without pause.

Now I have sung to You,

But still to no avail.

If You sang to me,

I surely could not fail.'[5]

---

[5] Book 2:5; Galvani, pp. 36-37.

She declares, "I have seen the one I love with the enlightened eyes of my soul."[6] Mechthild chooses to express her feelings in the first person which certainly reveal the "immediacy and truth."[7] In prayers, Mechthild understands God as immediately present. Again, this immediacy of the relationship is the source of her knowledge of God. Mechthild claims that she gained understanding of God, the intimacy between soul and God, through her many visions that God graciously granted to her.

---

[6] Book 2.2; Galvani pp. 29-30.

[7] Frank Tobin, *Mechthild von Magdeburg: A Medieval Mystic in Modern Eyes*, p. 44

Knowing God in Visions

As early as at the age of twelve, Mechthild began to experience vision. She believed in her own visions and she presents them in her book. They show how she was a spectator of many events. Her vivid description of heaven, hell and purgatory[1] are most striking. Heaven and hell represented feast and famine to her. Heaven is the Eucharistic feast of Christ's body and blood in the form of wafers and wine and Hell is a famine where the souls are literally stewed in pitches.[2] She watches "saints and disciples, the virgin and angelic orders celebrate Mass, and she sees Lucifer and his minions and their disgusting ways."[3] She sees how sister Hildegund is adorned in heaven with cloaks, with seven crowns, and how the nine choirs praised her.[4]

Mechthild presents her eschatological thought in Book 4.27 and Book 6.15. According to Thomas Benjamin deMayo, her vision suggests her expectation of a perfect mendicant life. Further, her description of the suffering of Enoch and Elijah at the hands of Antichrist highlights the religious traits such as suffering, martyrdom, holiness and communion with God.

---

[1] Book 3.21; Galvani, pp. 86-91.
[2] See, Susan Clark, "Introduction", *Flowing Light of Divinity*, p. xix.
[3] *Ibid*.
[4] Book 1.20; Galvani, pp. 44-45.

Benjamin deMayo argues that the purpose of presenting eschatological visions is to promote holiness in her own life and in the readers.[5] Likewise, her vision of the Trinity suggests that redemption is in the eternal plan of God and that God created humankind out of love and for a loving union with God.

This conversation within the Trinity explains how the Trinity descended to redeem humanity from sin so that the loving relationship between God and humanity can be renewed.

> Alas, then the Eternal Son kneeled before His Father and said: 'Dear Father, I will, if You will give me Your blessing. I will gladly accept bleeding mankind and anoint its wounds with the blood of My innocence. I will bandage man's wounds with the cloth of miserable degradation until I die. I will repay You, beloved Father, with human death for man's sin. Then the Holy Spirit said to the Father: 'O, almighty God, we will have a beautiful procession and will descend from these heights in great unmingled glory. I have, after all, been Mary's servant.' At that the Father leaned in great love toward the wills of the two and said to the Holy Spirit: 'You shall carry My light before My dear Son into the hearts of all whom He shall move with My words, and, Son, you shall take up Your cross. I will walk with You on all paths, and I will give You a pure virgin for a mother so that You might bear ignoble humanity more nobly.' The beautiful procession descended with great joy into the temple of Solomon, where almighty God wanted to take shelter for nine months.[6]

Mechthild's visions reveal God's intention to establish a loving relationship with His creation. They show the highest quality of intimacy with God as well as intellectual vigour. Her book

---

[5] For a detailed analysis, see Thomas Benjamin deMayo, "Mechthild of Magdeburg's Mystical Eschatology", *Journal of Medieval History*, 25, no. 2 (1999), 87-95.

[6] Book 3.9; Galvani, pp. 73-76, pp. 75-76.

is described as "the oldest and highest quality book of visions in German."[7] Two things can be noticed in her visions: Her close proximity with God (for in Book 2.20 she says that she was either lifted up to heaven or heaven came down to her) and personal conversation. Peter Dinzelbacher calls her visions "vision interviews."[8] In her visions, she asks theological questions and the figure that appears to her answers her questions.[9] Like Mechthild, Hadewijch of Antwerp, Hildegard and Gertrude of Helfta are all active participants in their visions. Gertrude speaks to Christ in her visions, asks questions and makes requests to Christ to intervene in certain matters that she is concerned about. She is also said to have received responses.[10]

The knowledge of God happens in the intensity of the visionary's relationship to God or the inner vision of God. Mechthild speaks of such knowledge as the knowledge of the Trinity. She celebrates and honours the Trinity which was revealed to her in her vision in such love and divine glow. She says,

> There in heavenly bliss I beheld with my soul's eyes the beautiful humanity of Our Lord Jesus Christ, and in His glorious countenance I recognized the Holy Trinity, the Father's eternity, and the Son's labor, and the sweetness of the Holy spirit.[11]

---

[7] Frank Tobin, *Mechthild von Magdeburg: A Medieval Mystic in Modern Eyes*, p. 96.

[8] Peter Dinzelbacher, *Vision und Visionsliteratur im Mittelalter*, Stuttgart: Hiersemann, 1981, pp. 144-45 cited in Frank Tobin, *Mechthild von Magdeburg: A Medieval Mystic in Modern Eyes*, p.114.

[9] *Ibid.*

[10] Grace M. Jantzen, *Power, Gender and Christian Mysticism* (Cambridge: Cambridge University Press, 1995), p. 164.

[11] Book 4, 2; Galvani, pp. 95-100, p. 96.

Her soul beheld the Trinity and was greeted by the Trinity in a courtly language. "He dresses her in clothes fit to be worn in a palace, and puts Himself at her disposal."[12] The soul is uplifted by God and the soul in her elevation enjoys the pleasure of knowing God. The soul experiences knowledge of God in deep intimacy. God fills poor, sterile souls with new knowledge, new visions, bringing strange pleasure in a new presence.

In Margot Schmidt's view, Mechthild relies both on tradition and her own spiritual experience when she writes about the Trinity. The union with the Trinity is described in erotic language.[13] In Book 1.5 she writes,

> If he seeks her, she flows to Him. She cannot contain herself, and He takes her to Himself. She would like to speak, but she cannot – so involved is she with the unity of the Holy Trinity. He gives her a little so that she may desire more. ...[14]

In the depth of love and close bond between the soul and the Lord, the Lord is known. Thus, God's knowledge burns within the soul. It glows within her in the intimacy of love. This suggests that the intimacy of love itself is knowledge. She wishes that the knowledge that happens in the intimate love experience would last a little longer. However, this sweet experience eludes her. She feels the pain of losing this

---

[12] Book 1.2; Galvani, pp. 6-8, p.6.

[13] Margot Schmidt, "'die spilende minnevluot,' Der Eros als Sein und Wirkkraft in der Trinitat bei Mechthild von Magdeburg", in *"Eine Höhe über die nichts geht": Spezielle Glaubenserfahrung in der Frauenmystik?* Ed. Margot Schmidt and Dieter R. Bauer, Stuttgart-Bad Cannstatt: Frommann-Holzboog, 1986, pp. 71-133, p. 78, cited in Frank Tobin, *Mechthild von Magdeburg: A Medieval Mystic in Modern Eyes*, pp. 97-98.

[14] Galvani, pp. 9-10, p. 10.

experience abruptly. But that is not all. God pursues the soul, captures her and binds her and unites her with him.[15]

In Mechthild's perception, God takes the initiative in bringing new knowledge to the soul. This is the experience of Gertrude too. God says to Gertrude in one of her visions: "I penetrate your entire being like ointment by the sweetness of my spirit...that you may grow in sanctity and aptitude for eternal life."[16] God secretly teaches the soul how to love and to grow in the perfection of love. The love in which knowing happens is God himself. Some Spanish male writers would also share this thought with Mechthild. For example, San Juan De La Cruz (1542-1591) calls this "an inflowing of God into the soul"[17]

Jeanne Ancelet-Hustache reports that there are three kinds of vision distinguished by theologians: visions apprehended through "the physical sense of sight," visions occurring through "internal images in the imagination" and visions occurring "purely in the intellect without any physical stimuli or internal images." But in Ancelet-Hustache's examination none of Mechthild's visions "involved the physical sense of sight" but, rather, they have the characteristic of seeing 'with the eyes of her soul." [18] These visions consist of internal images. As

---

[15] Book 1.3; Galvani, pp. 8-9. See also for the Trinitarian love of God Book 1.5; Galvani, pp. 9-10.

[16] Grace M. Jantzen, *Power, Gender and Christian Mysticism*, pp. 172-73, citing Caroline Walker Bynum, *Jesus as Mother: Studies in the Spirituality of the High Middle Ages* (Berkeley: University of California Press, 1984), p. 202.

[17] E. Allison Peers, *Spanish Mysticism: A Preliminary Survey* (London: Methuen, 1924), p. 111.

[18] Jeanne Ancelet-Hustache, Mechthild de Magdeburg (1207-1282): *Étude de psychologie religieuse*, Paris: Champion, 1926, p.134, cited in Frank Tobin, *Mechthild von Magdeburg: A Medieval Mystic in Modern Eyes*, p. 45.

Ancelet-Hustache's analysis shows, Mechthild's writings show that her visions contain internal images and Mechthild herself says that she sees with the eyes of her soul.

According to Bernard of Clairvaux (1091-1153), there are two kinds of vision, namely inner and external visions. The inner vision is not sensory. "It is beyond question that the vision is all the more delightful the more inward it is, and not external. It is the Word, who penetrates without sound; who is effective though not pronounced, who wins the affection without striking on the ears. His face, though without form, is the source of form, it does not dazzle the eyes of the body but gladdens the watchful heart.'"[19] Mechthild's visionary experiences fit well with Bernard's description of internal vision. Mechthild sees with the eyes of her soul and it does not lack an intellectual element. She perceives the Divine in her visions and re-presents them; she shows a good ability to interpret them and to be creative. Frank Tobin thinks "that a number of her descriptions force one to conclude that many of her visionary experiences, especially those connected with ecstasy, were purely intellectual in nature."[20] Tobin concludes that the medieval mystics might have been influenced by intellectual vision and used their own choice of words to describe them. Perhaps what becomes clear in their visions is that intellectual apprehension and exalted feeling are not separated. In this kind of knowing there is an integration of affective and cognitive dimensions. There is also an integration of particular and universal, since the visionary, here Mechthild, without losing her particular individual dimension, participates in the universal, the divine and the infinite dimension.

---

[19] Jerome Gellman, *Mystical Experience of God: A Philosophical Inquiry*, p. 7, citing Grace Jantzen, "Mysticism and Experience", *Religious Studies*, 25 (1989), p. 304.

[20] Frank Tobin, *Mechthild von Magdeburg: A Medieval Mystic in Modern Eyes*, p. 45.

It seems more plausible to think that they are speaking about an inner understanding that occurs in them along with visionary experiences. For example, Julian of Norwich presents a vision which explains how she gains understanding about God's love. She asks a question and she says that she was answered in her understanding. This is significant. The knowledge happens within. It is not a spoken word from outside but in the understanding that happens within her. She writes,

> And in this [God] showed me something small, no bigger than a hazelnut, lying in the palm of my hand, as it seemed to me, and it was as around as a ball. I looked at it with the eye of my understanding and thought: What can this be? I was amazed that it could last, for I thought that because of its littleness it would suddenly have fallen into nothing. And I was answered in my understanding: it lasts and always will, because God loves it, and thus everything has being through the love of God.[21]

Elizabeth Petroff in her work Medieval Women's Visionary Literature brings out another feature of medieval women's visionary experiences. She comments that retelling of a vision is a characteristic feature of medieval women's writing. She notes that Mechthild's visions are more like seeing a film and that they have two elements, namely, "visual iconography and dialogue." According to her, visions can be described as images and texts. In visions, the spiritual insights are seen in visible form. For this reason, visions are to be meditated upon and meanings are explored further.[22]

---

21 Julian of Norwich, *Showings*, Translated by Edmund Colledge and James Walsh, Classics of Western Spirituality (New York: Paulist, and London: SPCK, 1978), p.183, cited in Grace M. Jantzen, *Power, Gender and Christian Mysticism*, p.238.

22 Petroff, Elizabeth Alvilda, *Medieval Women's Visionary Literature* (New York: Oxford University Press, 1986), p.30, cited in Frank Tobin, *Mechthild von Magdeburg: A Medieval Mystic in Modern Eyes*, p. 104.

Susan Clark offers a graphic description of the nature of Mechthild's visions. She thinks that Mechthild's visions are reiterative rather than progressive since the same experience is told and re-told in many ways. She writes,

> Because of the episodic nature of her visions, Mechthild's revelations are not progressional but rather reiterative. What this amounts to in her case is that the same stories are told again and again, but with variations. Mystical union becomes interpreted sexually or chastely, with eagerness or reluctance, with penetration and withdrawal, with flowingness and aridity, ever familiar and yet ever new, and her descriptions are paradoxically homely and exalted.[23]

The manifestations of the supernatural realm occur in the world of common everyday experiences; and they are repeated and their visions are centred around a heavenly personality who brings a message from the heavenly realm. They are familiar yet ever new. The effect of such visions is to bring personal edification to the one who receives and to others who read such recorded visions.

The visions of Mechthild centre around God the Trinity who is the creator of humanity and who wishes to be in a loving relationship with humanity. In Jeanne Ancelet-Hustache's view, the subjects such as Trinity, Creator-creature and redemption are treated with a certain degree of pre-determination. The plan conceived by God before time was carried out in time in the Annunciation, the Nativity, Epiphany, Passion and Resurrection. Ancelet-Hustache surmises that Mechthild must have been influenced by the apocryphal gospels and the visual arts of her time. Mechthild's writings on the final days and last judgement show her influence of Apocalyptic thought. Furthermore she comments that one can observe "a very interesting mixture of popular piety and more abstract

---

[23] Susan Clark, "Introduction", *Flowing Light of Divinity*, p. xix.

meditation."[24] The foregoing discussion reveals some of the major features of Mechthild's visionary experience such as her intimacy with God and personal dialogue with God. In her vision experiences, she transcended the particular and was able to see and experience the depth dimension of the Divine. In other words, the truths of the depth dimension of the infinite were revealed in the visions.

She reinforces that she sees with the eyes of her soul and she presents her visions in order to promote piety, holiness and an intimate knowledge of God. Her visionary experiences are disclosive and transformative for her and by presenting them in her creative moment, she wishes the same to happen to her readers. Hence, her experiences effect both her own self-building and building up others. Religious women in the middle ages recorded their visions for common good, that is, for teaching purposes. Like Mechthild, another Beguine, Hadewijch, recorded a series of visions, which probably occurred to her when she was quite young, in order to instruct the young Beguines. Similarly, Julian of Norwich claims that she writes for comfort and spiritual assistance and encouragement. She addressed male and female religious people, clerics and lay leaders. All these religious women of the medieval age had one goal in common, that is to seek union with God alone and this is encouraged and promoted to their readers through their writings.

---

[24] Jeanne Ancelet-Hustache, Mechtilde de Magdeburg (1207-1282): *Étude de psychologie religieuse*, p. 187, cited in Frank Tobin, *Mechthild von Magdeburg: A Medieval Mystic in Modern Eyes*, p. 46.

Knowing God in Union

The soul longs for God and God longs for the soul and "when two fervent desires come together, love is perfected."[1] There is a union of God with the soul.[2] The word union is used by Mechthild for the culmination of love between the soul and God where the soul is natured in God. Hadewijch often speaks of this experience as 'having fruition of love.' She states,

'Since you, O Love, can do all with love,

Give me, for the sake of love, the fruition

That delights the loving soul through your highest goodness!'[3]

Hadewijch also explains fruition as 'being made God with God.' She says,

I desired to have full fruition of my Beloved, and to understand and taste him to the full. I desired that his Humanity should to the fullest extent be one in fruition with my humanity, and ...I wished he might content me interiorly with his Godhead, in one spirit, and that for me he should be all that he is, without withholding anything from me...For

---

[1] Book 7.16; Galvani, p. 221.

[2] Book 6.23; Galvani, p. 193.

[3] Hadewijch, *The Complete Works*, translated and introduction by Mother Columbia Hart, Classics of Western Spirituality Series (New York: Paulist, and London: SPCK, 1986), p. 236, cited in Grace M. Jantzen, *Power, Gender and Christian Mysticism*, p. 135.

that is the most perfect satisfaction: to grow up in order to be God with God.[4]

For Hadewijch and Mechthild alike union is the delight of the soul and the highest goodness. It is an immediate experience, an intense feeling of love and of the presence of God. Here, the union of the soul with the divine or the union of a lover with the beloved is one without confusion of identity. It is not absorption or annihilation of individuality but rather a banishment of otherness.

It is bliss to be united with God. It is the drunken joy of Bliss in the Godhead that is beyond earthly joy.[5] But this bliss is possible to the soul that is pure. Mechthild, very strongly condemns sin since God is known only by the sinless soul. Sin prevents us from reaching God. The knowledge of God comes from God Himself to the soul that is pure. The soul has to keep herself from all sins so that she will not detract from perfection.[6] Human sin robs the soul of intimacy with God and leads us into the eternal abyss.[7]

In Mechthild's view, Adam and Eve were created pure and sinless with incorruptible bodies, but they became sinful and lost their incorruptible bodies. The fallen body has the tendency to sin. However, the soul retains its original likeness to God and strives to ascend to God.[8] Pride, disobedience, wicked cupidity, gluttony, lasciviousness, anger, falseness, manslaughter, lying betrayal and despair – these are not

---

[4] Hadewijch, *The Complete Works*, p. 280, cited in Grace M. Jantzen, *Power, Gender and Christian Mysticism*, p. 140.

[5] Book 7.7; Galvani, pp. 215-217.

[6] Book 5.33; Galvani, pp. 161-162. p. 162.

[7] Book 3.7; Galvani, p. 72; Book 4.5; Galvani, pp. 104-105; Book 4.6; Galvani, p. 106; Book 3.9; Galvani, pp. 73-76.

[8] Rosemary Radford Ruether, *Visionary Women: Three Medieval Mystics*, pp. 35-36.

tolerated and they are to be punished.[9] However, real remorse is pardoned by God in God's grace.[10] Mechthild seems to stress that one needs the grace and the aid of God to keep oneself filled with truth. She does speak of merit but she seems to think that good works are not sufficient and therefore speaks of an attributed justification.[11]

Dishonesty, falsehood, deception, speaking greedy, haughty words from an angry heart would result in losing the sweet intimacy of God. One can guard oneself from such vile only if there is a deep-rooted awareness that God looks into one's heart.[12] Mechthild claims that this book is called '*A Flowing Light of My Divinity*' since the divinity flows "into the hearts of all those who live without falsehood."[13]

Mechthild suggests a way of prayer and confession to God everyday.

I, sinful creature,

I lament and confess to God all of my sins

Of which I am guilty in His eyes

I confess and lament all the good deeds

which I have omitted

I confess and lament all the sins I committed

Before I knew what sin was

I lament those sins even more

That I committed with knowledge

---

[9] See, Book 3.1; Galvani, pp. 86-91, pp. 86-87.

[10] See, Book 4.6; Galvani, pp. 106-107, p. 106.

[11] Frank Tobin, *Mechthild von Magdeburg: A Medieval Mystic in Modern Eyes*, p. 29.

[12] See, Book 5. 22; Galvani, pp. 144-145. p. 145.

[13] See, Galvani, p. 5.

With anger, restlessness, and with vanity

'Take pity on me, Lord,

For I am truly sorry for them

And grant me, Lord, Your full assurance

That You have forgiven me them all;

I cannot otherwise live with joy.

Jesus my beloved,

Let me come to You

In true remorse

And heartfelt love

And never let me grow cold,

So that I might always feel

Your heartfelt love

In my heart, in my soul,

In my five senses

And in all my limbs;

Then I can never grow cold.'[14]

The sinless soul knows God within and experiences union with the Divine. Eternity is "the uncreated wisdom of the everlasting Divinity."[15] Sometimes, Mechthild speaks of eternity as the immediate experience with God. It may be for a brief moment which can be repeated if God wishes. Mechthild writes of her own experience and it makes it possible to understand that in her experience, an immediate knowledge of God is the same as union with the divine.

> This is a greeting with many streams; forever it breaks forth from the flowing God into poor, sterile souls with new knowledge, new visions, bringing strange pleasure in a new

---

14 Book 7.38; Galvani, pp. 243-44.
15 Book 7.1; Galvani, pp. 207-211, p. 207.

presence. Alas, dear God, burning within and glowing without, now that You have given this to the least of souls, I was able to experience this life You have given to the worthier souls; that is why I wanted to absorb this experience a little longer. ...[16]

The following conversation between the youth and the soul explains how the soul is satisfied with God alone and that knowing God and being united with him alone is eternal life. This comes from God to the soul by God's own initiative.

'Lord, now I am a naked soul,

And You, in Yourself, a beautifully adorned God.

Our communion

Is eternal life without death.'

Then ensued a blessed quiet,

According to both their wishes.

He gives Himself to her and she to Him,

And only she knows what happens to her at this moment,

And that is good enough for me.

Now things cannot remain like this for long.

When two lovers meet in secret

They must take leave of each other undivided.

'Dear friend in God, this path in love I have written for you.

It is God Who must place it into your heart.

Amen.'[17]

William Kimbrel comments that Mechthild uses courtly love poem's form, language and imagery and adapts them to a Christian scenario. With this Christian adaptation, they attain

---

[16] Book 1.2; Galvani, pp. 6-8, pp. 7-8.
[17] Book 1.44; Galvani, pp. 22-26, p. 26.

an act of consummation which is denied in its own context.[18] In Mechthild's writings, the path of love and the desire to seek God intimately and the longing for blissful union is given by God Himself to the soul.

The blissful union is between God and the soul. The body is not included in this ecstatic experience. She seems to accept the platonic division between body and soul and the supremacy of soul over body. Her detest of the body is expressed thus: The soul is the bride and the "the Bride has a pack animal, which is the body; it is bridled with unworthiness; degradation is its fodder, and its stable the confessional. The burden which it bears is innocence."[19] Hence, "the soul departs from the body with all its might, wisdom, love and longing..."[20]

In one of her visions, she tells how the soul enjoys the immeasurable pleasure of knowing the beloved deeply. "He pulls her along to a secret place, and there she must not ask for anyone, for He wants to play a game with her alone, a game not known to the body."[21] When the game is at the peak or at the point of culmination, God says to the soul that she must descend. The following dialogue expresses her misery at having to leave God and join her body.

> And so the radiant God speaks: 'Maiden, you must descend.' And she is frightened as she says: 'O Lord, now You have taken me so far that no command can make me praise You when I am in my body; instead I must suffer miserably and struggle against my body.' He says: 'Alas, My beloved dove, your voice is like music to My ears, your words are like herbs

---

[18] Kimbrel Jr., William W. "Mechthild of Magdeburg: The Transformational Character of Mystical Poetry",*Massachusetts Studies in English*, 6 (1972), 47-57, pp. 55-56, cited in Frank Tobin, *Mechthild von Magdeburg: A Medieval Mystic in Modern Eyes*, pp. 64-65.

[19] Book 1.46; Galvani, pp. 26-28, p. 27.

[20] Book 1.2; Galvani, pp. 6-8. p. 6.

[21] *Ibid.*

> in My mouth, your longing is the richness of My gift.' And
> she answers: 'Dear Lord, the guest must heed the wishes of
> the host.'
>
> She sighs so deeply that the body awakes. The body says:
> 'Mistress, where have you been? You return so lovely,
> beautiful and strong, free and sensitive. The change in you
> has taken away all my appetite, all my pleasure, my color,
> and all my power.' She replies: 'Be silent, murderer; stop your
> lamenting. From now on I will be on my guard against you.
> The wounding of my foe does not disturb me; it delights
> me.'[22]

There is a separation of body from soul in ecstasy. In ecstasy,
the body exists "as in a sweet sleep."[23] In Schmidt's view three
levels of elevation of the soul can be found in Mechthild's
writings.

> On the first level the soul is completely in God's power and
> he grants all its wishes. The soul remains active and in
> possession of all its spiritual faculties. On the second level
> the soul is in a hidden place deeper within the divinity where
> God determines everything and the soul is more passive and
> receptive. On the third and highest level the soul inhabits a
> 'blissful place' where, in its amazement, it loses all memory
> of life on earth.[24]

Thus, "in ecstatic experience the soul temporarily frees itself
from its ties to the body and tastes its original and renewed
love relation with God, which has been lost with the fall but
restored through the incarnation of Christ in Mary's sinless
flesh."[25] Mechthild thinks that what Eve lost was conquered

---

[22] Book 1.2; Galvani, pp. 6-8, p. 7.

[23] Book 1.2; Galvani, pp. 7-8.

[24] Margot Schmidt, "Elemente der Schau bei Mechthild von Magdeburg
und Mechthild von Hackeborn: Zur Bedeutung der geistlichen Sinne,"
in *Frauenmystik im Mittelalter* (1985), 123-51, pp. 126-27, cited in Frank
Tobin, *Mechthild von Magdeburg: A Medieval Mystic in Modern Eyes*, p.
97.

[25] Rosemary Radford Ruether, *Visionary Women: Three Medieval Mystics*,
p. 37.

by Mary. "Mary, whose body was uncorrupted, preserved this original love relation of the soul with God during the period between the fall of Adam and the incarnation. Mary, as God's bride, exemplifies what God intended, and continues to intend, the soul to be."[26] Mary speaks,

> 'So the almighty Father chose me for a Bride, in order to have something to love, for His beloved Bride, the noble soul, was dead.... Then I alone became Bride of the Holy Trinity and the Mother of orphans, and brought them before the eyes of God, so they might not sink.'[27]

In Mechthild's vision, however there is place for body, but for a redeemed body. In the eternal life, when the righteous soul lives with God eternally, the redeemed body experiences unending pleasure. It is all light and without darkness.mThe bliss of union that may be for a brief moment in this life will be a constant pleasure and unending happiness in the life after. As the soul experiences the blissful moment here on earth, she understands and knows God in the intimacy of the union. The knowledge is an experiential knowledge which is tasted by the soul alone in the union. However, union is not the only way to know God for Mechthild speaks repeatedly about being abandoned by God. Hence, alienation and separation from God and also abandonment by God become a way of knowing God.

---

[26] *Ibid.*

[27] Rosemary Radford Ruether, *Visionary Women: Three Medieval Mystics,* p. 37, citing Galvani, pp. 15-16.

Knowing God in Separation and Abandonment

Alienation from God is the central experience that is recounted in Mechthild's writing. She seems to feel heavily about the abandonment by God and expresses her need to receive the gift from God to remain true to God in her distress even when she is deprived of all consolation as a dog who is by nature remains true to its master.[1] She tells God, "how I long for You when You want to shun me." She expresses her pain in these words:

'All the other creatures dare not tell You

If they had to lament for me,

For I suffer inhuman distress;

A human death would be far gentler to me.

I seek You in my thoughts

Like a bride wooing her groom.

I suffer great illness

For being bound to You.

Since the bond is stronger than I,

I cannot free myself from love.

---

[1] Book 2.25; Galvani pp. 52-55; Book 2.4; Galvani, pp. 33-36.

I call out for You in my longing,

In a wretched voice.

I wait for You with a heavy heart;

I cannot rest, burning unextinguished

With flaming love for You.

I pursue You with all my might.

Had I the strength of a giant,

It would quickly vanish

If I came upon Your footprints.

Alas, my love, now do not run so far ahead of me,

And rest a little lovingly

That I may catch up with you.[2]

All for longing for You.

My flesh atrophies, my blood dries up,

My bones grow cold, my veins convulse,

And my heart dissolves with love for You,

And my soul burns like the roar of a hungry lion.

How will I be, and where are You?'[3]

Similarly, for Hadewijch, God offers himself but also withdraws. God loves but also abandons.

Hadewijch writes,

Sometimes afire and sometimes cold,

Sometimes cautious and sometimes reckless,

Love is full of fickleness.

---

2 Book 2.25, pp. 52-55, pp. 52-3.
3 Book 2.25, pp. 52-55, p. 54.

Love summons us all

To pay our great debt

for her rich power,

which she invites us to share.

Sometimes gracious and sometimes fierce,

Sometimes aloof and sometimes close by:

For him who understands this in fidelity to Love

It is a matter for jubilation:

how Love knocks down

And seizes

At one stroke.

Sometimes stooping low and sometimes mounting high,

sometimes hidden and sometimes revealed:

Before Love cherishes anyone,

He suffers many adventures

Ere he arrives

where he tastes

The nature of Love.[4]

Hadawijch images God in terms of Lady Love. In courtly romance between the Lady Love and the male knight, the withdrawal and absence of the Lady become too painful to bear. Hadewijch complains,

Sweet as Love's nature is,

Where can she come by the strange hatred

With which she continually pursues me

---

4 Hadewijch, *The Complete Works*, p. 140, cited in Grace M. Jantzen, *Power, Gender and Christian Mysticism*, pp. 292-93.

And transpierces the depths of my heart with storm?

I wander in darkness without clarity,

Without liberating consolation, and in strange fear.[5]

For Mechthild, the soul that is separated from the beloved cannot be consoled by any other means. She can be consoled only by God. In Book 1.44, the senses offer the soul the consolation of the chastity of virgins and other delights but the soul rejects them. The soul even rejects the experience of Mary's motherhood of suckling the infant Jesus saying that it is but a child's love. The soul can only be satisfied by an adult love offered by her lover. When the senses caution the soul that the experience of the union with the lover will overwhelm the soul, the soul answers, saying,

Fish will not drown in water,

Birds will not sink in air.

God will not spoil in fire;

For it is there that it obtains its true and brilliant color.

God has given to all His creatures

The gift of making use of their talents.

How can I fight my nature?

I should forfeit all to go to God

Who is my Father by nature,

My brother by His Humanity,

My Bridegroom by Love,

And I am His since the beginning of time.

Do you not wish me to experience my nature?[6]

---

[5] Hadewijch, *The Complete Works*, p. 229, cited in Grace M. Jantzen, *Power, Gender and Christian Mysticism*, p. 293.

[6] Book 1.44; Galvani, pp. 22-26, pp. 24-25.

The soul thus explains to the senses that she will not be overwhelmed by the union since she belongs to God the lover from the beginning of time. As the fish does not drown in water since its nature is to live in water, her nature is to be in love and she wishes to experience her nature.

The soul knows God in union and feels the separation. Yet, in separation she knows that nothing can satisfy but the beloved's presence. The more she endures the separation, the more she knows the true dwelling place of the beloved is within her heart. This is confirmed when she is once again united with God after a period of separation.

However, the soul feels God's abandonment and laments that God has cast it aside from his love. It is like a rich man who suffers great poverty after having enjoyed splendid wealth.[7] The loving soul expresses how painful it is to be severed from God. The mission of love is to link together the human soul and God. She speaks about the amazing wisdom of love.[8] Lady Love has the greatest power to fill empty hearts and the wisdom to unite lovers. Love does not have an end. Love's mission always has been, and still is, to link the lover and the loved. Mechthild sees Love as the link that unites God and the soul.[9]

When hearts are filled with strife and bitterness, love cannot carry on its mission. Here in the following poem, love is referred to as a lady and a queen. To be parted from God will be more painful than death. The soul requests Lady Love (Lady *Minne*) to prevent any separation from God whom she loves.

---

[7] Book 3.5; Galvani, pp. 70-71. See also, Book 3.6; Galvani, pp.71-72.
[8] Book 5.31; Galvani, pp. 160-61.
[9] Book 1.1; Galvani, pp. 5-6; Book 1.3; Galvani pp. 8-9.

O blessed love without end!

Your mission was and still is

To link God and the human soul together,

And that shall always be your mission.

Greetings, my lady,

And beware lest I complain

About you to my beautiful Lord.

If He wishes to be away from me too long

I would certainly freeze.

Please prevent that, lady of my heart, my queen!

You have led me to God

So that I am blissfully bound to Him.

O, My lady, please help me

To die in His arms

in which I am caught

yet I would gladly suffer the pain of death

In my sinful body.

Love, you have the greatest power

Above all virtues

I will thank God

That you take from me many heartaches

I have no more virtues;

He serves me with His.

It would be more difficult than death for me

To do any good without my Lord.

When I talk of love,

I dare not refer to myself

> Rather, God includes all those
>
> who are chosen ones of His heart.
>
> Those whom it concerns know it well;
>
> Love fills empty hearts
>
> When we grow full of strife and bitterness
>
> We are unprepared for the play of love.
>
> Good night, love, since I must sleep. Alleluia.[10]

Only by meeting the Lord and being kissed by him can the soul rise above herself. Only the lover and his kisses can heal the wound caused by separation from the lover.[11]

One can observe a similar malady of love and its pain in the writings of John of Cross. The pain can be alleviated only by the Beloved. John of the Cross writes,

> Behold, the malady of love is incurable, except in Thy presence and before they face. The reason why the malady of love admits of no other remedy than the presence and countenance of the Beloved is that the malady of love differs from every other sickness, and therefore requires a different remedy ... love is not cured but by that which is in harmony with itself. ... There is no remedy for this pain except in the presence and vision of the Beloved.[12]

Mechthild seems to think that God keeps away in order to increase her devotion. God's love makes the soul wise.[13] She experiences God in the bliss of the experience of union and also the pangs of separation. Some of her writings show that in fact she welcomes such alienation since it enables her to taste the depth of divine love. In Book 4.12 she writes,

---

[10] Book 4.19; Galvani, pp. 117-18.

[11] Book 2.15; Galvani, p. 40.

[12] Margaret Smith, p. 64, citing St. John of the Cross, *Spiritual Canticle*, pp. 54, 84, 85.

[13] Book 2.17; Galvani, p. 41.

Then the constant alienation from God came and enveloped the soul so much that the blessed soul said this: 'Welcome, blessed alienation. Happy am I that I was born and that you, lady, will be my lady-in-waiting, for you bring me unaccustomed joy and inconceivable wonders and even unbearable sweetness. But Lord, you must take this sweetness and let me experience alienation from You. Alas, happy am I, faithful God, that I must bear it after the transformation of love in the palate of my soul.

Alas, blessed alienation from God, how lovingly I am bound to you! You steady my will in pain and endear to me the hard long waiting in this poor body. The closer I come to you, the more wondrously God falls on me. O, Lord, even in the depth of unmingled humiliation I cannot sink away from You.[14]

She writes about how God touches His friends with pain,

When man has a sadness

which he does not comprehend,

When he is guilty of little sins,

The Lord says this: 'I have touched them.' Meaning:

'In the same way in which My Father allowed Me to be touched on earth,

Those whom I draw to Me,

The closer they come to Me

When man conquers himself,

Valuing pain and solace equally,

I will lift him up in sweetness,

And he shall taste Eternal Life.[15]

---

[14] Galvani, pp. 107-111, pp. 110-111.
[15] Book 7.56; Galvani, p. 260.

Love is not without pain. But the Lord declares, "In your pain, you are My lamb. In your sighs, you are My turtledove. In your waiting, you are My Bride."[16]

Pain is a way of understanding God's care and love. Alois Maria Haas, analysing Mechthild's writings on suffering, observes that for Mechthild "God descends more powerfully and strangely upon the creature, the deeper it is caught up and bound in alienation."[17] Thus, pain is a way of knowing God deeper.

Mechthild speaks of the likeness of the soul to God. When she speaks of suffering she seems to identify human suffering with the passion of Christ. She personally experienced deep sorrow and for her suffering is a way of knowing God. Suffering makes people holy. Mechthild's spirituality was shaped and nurtured by love for God and by suffering when she felt the absence of God, the lover.

---

[16] Book 1.34; Galvani, p. 19.

[17] Alois Maria Haas, "Mechthild von Magdeburg – Dichtung und Mystik," *Amsterdamer Beiträge zur älteren Germanistik*, 2 (1972), 105-56, p. 125, cited in Frank Tobin, *Mechthild von Magdeburg: A Medieval Mystic in Modern Eyes*, p. 67.

Knowing God in Participating in Christ's Suffering

Mechthild's focus was on suffering of Christ and Christians' willingness to suffer along with Christ. In Mechthild's writings, suffering turns love into a deed. Passion is a necessary part of loving Christ. Suffering is the way of imitation of Christ. It is living with God. In Book 5.2, she says, "whenever faithless people have overwhelmed me with suffering, God has comforted me thus by saying: "Look, no one can escape suffering, for hour by hour it cleanses man of his many sins."[1] Thus, suffering leads towards perfection. For this sake, Mechthild was ready to undergo any kind of suffering. The following dialogue shows that God himself chooses to afflict her with sickness so that she might know God's love and care:

> He asked me for my opinion: 'Now tell Me, you are Mine, are you not?' 'yes, Lord, that is what I long to be.' 'Can I not then do with you as I please?' 'Indeed, Beloved, and even if I were to be annihilated.' And Our Lord replied: 'You must follow and trust Me in these things, and you shall be ill for a long time. I Myself will care for you and give you all you need in body and soul.'[2]

---

[1] Galvani, pp. 130-31, p. 131.

[2] Book 4.2; Galvani, pp. 95-100.

God strikes and cares. Mechthild's physical illness becomes the medium whereby God reveals his compassion. It leads to knowing God's intimate care in suffering and thus gaining a knowledge of God in another dimension of life.

Elisabeth Schwarz-Mehrens points out that in Mechthild's writing, suffering becomes 'the norm and direction for the love of God.'[3] Margit Sinka says that for Mechthild, Christ's wounds are significant in reaching Christ. It is part of her Christ-centred spirituality.[4] Christ's suffering enables her to understand as well as cope with her own sufferings of different sorts. She finds her Beloved in the very place of her own suffering. Suffering is a way of knowing and uniting with the Beloved since she treads the same path as her Beloved and drinks the same wine he himself drank.[5]

The following conversation between Christ and the soul explains that human suffering is a way towards perfection and to participating in Christ's suffering.

> 'Lord, You are forever wounded for love of me,
>
> You have proven that to me.
>
> You have written me in the book of Your divinity.
>
> You have depicted me in Your humanity.
>
> You have buried me at Your side

---

3 Schwarz-Mehrens, Elisabeth, *Zum Funktionieren und zur Funktion der Compassio im Fließenden Licht der Gottheit Mechthilds von Magdeburg,* Göppingen: Kümmerle, 1985, p. 205, cited in Frank Tobin, *Mechthild von Magdeburg: A Medieval Mystic in Modern Eyes,* p. 101.

4 Frank Tobin, *Mechthild von Magdeburg: A Medieval Mystic in Modern Eyes,* p. 102, citing Margit Sinka, "Christological Mysticism in Mechthild von Magdeburg's Das *fleißende* Licht der Gottheit: A Journey of Wounds" *Germanic Review,* 60 (1985), 123-28.

5 Michelle Voss Roberts, "Flowing and Crossing: The Somatic Theologies of Mechthild and Lalleśwari ", *Journal of the American Academy of Religion,* 76, no. 3 (2008), 638-663, p. 665.

By my hands and feet.
Alas, please allow me, Beloved,
To anoint You.'
'But where, my love, will you find the ointment?'
'Lord, I would tear my heart in two
And place You in it.
You could never give me so precious an anointing
As that I might forever soar in Your heart.
Lord, if You would take me home with You,
I would forever be Your physician.'
'Yes, I will, but My loyalty must ask you to wait;
My love asks you to work;
My patience asks you to be silent;
My sorrow asks you to suffer poverty;
My degradation asks you to bear it;
My longing asks you not to lament;
My victory asks you to pursue all virtues;
My death asks you to endure many things.
In all that you will have honor
Until I unburden you of your great load.'[6]

In suffering the soul experiences not only union with the Beloved but also a painful waiting. However, the soul endures suffering, patience, degradation and remains in poverty until she is accepted by God again. Suffering enables the soul to be patient, enduring and persevering until the day of honour is at hand. Mechthild's hope is that all the faithful souls will be united with God and there will be no more lamentations. This is the blessed hope of obedient souls.

---

[6] Book 3.2; Galvani, pp. 66-67.

Knowing God in Mission

Mechthild was a woman of action. Love without knowledge and profession without practice is not encouraged in Mechthild's writing.

Love without knowledge,

The wise soul believes, is darkness.

Profession without practice

She believes to be the pain of Hell.

With practice that leads to death she cannot find fault.[1]

She asks "of what use are elevated words without deeds done out of compassion?"[2] And she states,

...Beautiful vows without faithful deeds,

That is falsehood and the Devil's counsel. ...[3]

Through action or in doing, Mechthild attains knowledge. In other words, in the praxis, Mechthild learns of love, learns of God. It is a method of knowing by doing. Love begins with virtues. Hadewijch likewise speaks of learning love through practising love. God tells her that when she has learned what

---

[1] Book 1.21; Galvani, pp. 13-14.
[2] Book 6.30; Galvani, p. 197.
[3] Book 3.14; Galvani, pp. 80-81.

love is, through practising love, then she will be love as the Lord is Love.[4]

We understand from Mechthild's writings that she was probably engaged in helping the sick and the poor and in praying for others. For Beguines, religion itself was a performance. They "incorporated activities and elaborated prayers around life-size pietas." They often engaged in "detailed reflections on and participation in Eucharistic rituals."[5]

Most importantly, Mechthild often speaks of her responsibility as a Christian in praying for others.[6] Peter Dinzelbacher thinks that Mechthild was so perfected in her spirit and closeness with God that her personal feeling and relationship to God proffer spiritual benefits and spiritual assistance to others. The spiritual benefits such as alms-giving, masses or prayers depend on the charismatic person's relationship with God. "It is the personal relationship of the charismatic person that moves God to bestow this special favour; it is their feeling– and no longer the deed that brings about redemption."[7] The thoughts of some of the Spanish writers might further explain the importance of prayer in a religious person. Francisco De Osuna (-c. 1540), speaking about prayer, says that the presence of God makes itself felt quietly to the loving soul, secretly, in a hidden way and it is perceived

---

[4] Grace M. Jantzen, *Power, Gender and Christian Mysticism*, pp. 141-42, citing Hadewijch, *The Complete Works*, p. 272.

[5] Patricia Zimmerman Beckman, "The Power of Books and the Practice of Mysticism in the Fourteenth Century: Heinrich Nördlingen and Margaret Ebner on Mechthild's Flowing Light of the Godhead", see notes 25 and 26 on p. 69.

[6] Book 3.17; Galvani, pp. 83-84; Book 3.18; Galvani, pp. 84-85; Book 6.37; Galvani, pp. 202-204; Book 7.2, Galvani, pp. 211-213.

[7] Peter Dinzelbacher, *Vision und Visionsliteratur im Mittelalter*, p. 159, cited in Frank Tobin, *Mechthild von Magdeburg: A Medieval Mystic in Modern Eyes*, pp. 114-15.

in the smallest whisper.[8] No words could be more comprehensive, collective and spiritual than the words of the soul said inwardly 'I am his and he is mine.'[9] This kind of knowing within the self transforms the very idea of prayer. Who is praying? The soul or the Lord himself? There is conformity between the one who prays and the Lord to whom he or she prays or the Lord who hears his or her prayer.[10]

Likewise, San Pedro De Alcantara (1499-1562) explains that within one's self, in the centre of one's soul, is the image of God. It is here that speaking and listening take place. But such speaking or prayer and listening (the Lord who listens) become one. The one who prays does not remember that he or she is praying.[11]

The soul is the temple of God. Luis De Leòn (1528-1591) clarifies that it is the Trinity which resides in the soul for Christ says 'he that loves me shall be loved by my Father and we will come and make our abode in him.'[12] Eternity is in one's own soul. Everlasting life is possible here and now. When the soul conquers all evil she knows marvellous purity and fecundity.[13]

Mechthild, along with the significance of prayer, speaks about a cosmic vision. Her cosmic vision is derived from her Trinitarian understanding of God and God's mission in the cosmos. The Holy Trinity touches everyone, whether rich or poor. The Holy Ghost by moving through the whole of creation brings eternal joy. The loving humanity of Christ greets people with brotherly companionship.

---

[8] E. Allison Peers, *Spanish Mysticism: A Preliminary Survey*, p. 73.

[9] *Ibid.*, pp. 69-70.

[10] *Ibid.*, p. 73.

[11] E. Allison Peers, *Spanish Mysticism: A Preliminary Survey*, p. 84.

[12] *Ibid.*, pp. 160-61.

[13] *Ibid.*, p. 137.

From the noblest crossbow of the Holy Trinity,

From the divine throne through the nine choirs.

Everyone, whether rich or poor,

Is struck lovingly;

All are shot by the rays of the Divinity

With an incredible brightness.

Loving humanity greets them

With brotherly companionship.

The Holy Ghost moves them by flowing through them

With wondrous creations

Of eternal joy.

The undivided God feeds them

With the glance of His splendid countenance

And fills them with the eager breath

Of His flowing mouth.

And as they move with ease through the air,

Like birds, though no feathers touch them,

They go where they wish.[14]

An egalitarian communal life is valued in her writings. She took the role upon herself as a mediator between God and creatures. She saw her mission as intervening between God and people. By being a mediator and intercessor she models herself on Mary the intercessor. She speaks about the teaching wisdom of Mary, and sees Mary as a helper to widows, a refuge for sinners, an honour to all the saints, a strong helper of the despondent, an intercessor for the whole world.[15] Like Mary,

---

[14] Book 2.3; Galvani, pp. 30-33, p. 31.
[15] Book 7.19; Galvani, pp. 224-225.

she saw herself linking the realms of the human and divine. William Kimbrel sees her as a point of contact between meditation and transformation, the unconscious and the conscious mind.[16] Likewise, Haas thinks that Mechthild becomes a point of mediation between God and the world.

Mechthild attacked the corruption in the church and the faults of the clergy.[17] She was able to discern the hypocrisy and self-centredness of the clergy who being far from the true spiritual life corrupt others.[18] She "locates several dishonest prelates and wretched priests in purgatory, where they are fished out, filleted, boiled, eaten, and then defecated by devils."[19]

A friend and an enemy are treated equally. Justice to enemies as well as to friends, mercy in distress, loyalty in companionship, giving assistance and goodwill are rendered equally to friends and foes.[20] Mechthild believed that the works of good people reflect upon the works of our Lord.[21] Voluntary poverty is praised as one of the virtues along with good will, truth, wisdom, strength and righteousness.[22] At this point, one

---

[16] William W. Kimbrel Jr., "Mechthild of Magdeburg: The Transformational Character of Mystical Poetry", p. 47, cited in Frank Tobin, *Mechthild von Magdeburg: A Medieval Mystic in Modern Eyes*, p. 64.

[17] See, Frank Tobin, *Mechthild von Magdeburg: A Medieval Mystic in Modern Eyes*, p. 124.

[18] Rosemary Radford Ruether, *Visionary Women: Three Medieval Mystics*, p. 33.

[19] Patricia Zimmerman Beckman, "The Power of Books and the Practice of Mysticism in the Fourteenth century: Heinrich of Nördlingen and Margaret Ebner on Mechthild's Flowing Light of the Godhead", note 35, on p. 72.

[20] See, Book 5.22; Galvani, pp. 144-45, p.144.

[21] Book 7.32; Galvani, p. 235.

[22] See, Book 2. 20; Galvani, pp. 44-45; Book 4.22; Galvani, pp. 119-121. The idea of voluntary poverty was seen in general in the medieval religious men and women. Further, voluntary poverty, casting off

cannot forget St. Francis of Assisi who can be acclaimed as the epitome of poverty. He stripped himself naked and married Lady Poverty for the sake of Christ. He taught his followers to ask nothing for themselves and in so doing, poverty is bound to follow. Once when a poor woman came for alms, Francis gave the New Testament, the only possession he had at that time, to the woman so that she could sell it for necessity.[23] In Franciscan practice of voluntary poverty, the whole world is considered as a cloister. There is a change in the way this practice understood the relationship between the world and the cloister.[24] Clare of Assisi who was drawn to Francis's vision, and her community, 'Poor Clares' or 'Poor Ladies'; lived a radical life of poverty. The sisters of the community were referred to not as reclusae or recluses of the world but rather as inclusae who were in the world and served the world.[25] Mechthild could not be compared to St Francis of Assisi but she had the ardent desire to embrace poverty so that she may partake in Christ's suffering and poverty. This *imitatio Christi* is a way of knowing Christ and obtaining the knowledge of Christ.

Her belief that the coming age of the spirit will be different since it will be accomplished by "a new order of priests" reveals

---

worldly wealth and riches for the sake of Christ dominated late medieval religious thought and this interacted largely with religious reform and spiritual renewal. See, Michael D. Bailey, "Religious Poverty, Mendicancy and Reform in the Late Middle Ages", *Church History*, 72, no. 3 (2003), pp. 457-483.

[23] John R. H. Moorman, *Saint Francis of Assisi* (London: SPCK, 1963), pp. 20-42. See also, Margaret Smith, *Muslim Women Mystics: The Life and Work of Rabia and other Women Mystics in Islam* (Oxford: One world, 2001), pp. 91-92; 98-99.

[24] Bernard McGinn, "The Changing Shape of Late Medieval Mysticism", p. 199.

[25] Roger Schroeder, "Women, Mission and the Early Franciscan Movement", p. 414.

her love of "freedom from stereotyped religious patterns." In a sense she anticipated a "transition from an order that was sacral and hierarchical to one that was becoming liberal, with emphasis on the human individual "[26]

She had a cosmic view of the history of salvation; history that embraces the origin of the world, fall and redemption and the apocalyptic end of time and life beyond. Her mystical vision does not lose sight of this cosmic view. Balthasar points out that Mechthild calls her "relationship to the cosmos and history of salvation existential because her own longings are expanded to coincide with their dimensions."[27] Further, this historical view enabled her to see herself ministering to the whole world. Tobin comments, "Mechthild's soul, living in the flowing divine light, is universal, catholic. Her duties are global and she lives for the world as mother of souls. Her sufferings have redemptive value; she intercedes for sinners; her prayers embrace the whole divine order."[28]

Hence, her spirituality went beyond the inner experience with God and stretched out to others in active loving mission. In Mechthild's view, the loveliest thing to be found in a human being is the love of God expressed in actions. In this lie "the noblest joy of the senses" and "the holiest peace of the heart."[29]

---

[26] Emilie Zum Brunn and Gerorgette Epiney-Burgard, *Women Mystics in Medieval Europe* (New York: Paragon, 1989), p. 52, cited in Grace M. Jantzen, *Power, Gender and Christian Mysticism*, pp. 105-6.

[27] Hans Urs von Balthasar, "Mechthilds Kirchlicher Auftrag", in Margot Schmidt's translation of Das flie Licht der Gottheit, Dissertation, Freiburg University, 1955, p.28, citied in Frank Tobin, Mechthild von Magdeburg: A Medieval Mystic in Modern Eyes, p.61.

[28] Frank Tobin, *Mechthild von Magdeburg: A Medieval Mystic in Modern Eyes*, p. 62.

[29] See, Book 5.22; Galvani, pp. 44-45, p. 44.

Part - II
An Appraisal

Mechthild's Work:
A Woman's Contribution to the
Way of Knowing God

A Female Voice

Mechthild wrote at a time when the Church was seen as the authoritative body which had true access to the knowledge and the mysteries of God. The male ecclesiastical hierarchy defined what constituted knowledge.[1] In the context of male supremacy that dominated the church and society, women writers in the medieval age spoke, wrote and established their authority in the midst of interconnected struggles of power and gender. In this context it does not come as a surprise that the veracity of Mechthild's visions and her right to make them public were challenged by her male counterparts.

Susan Clark describes Mechthild as a "fascinating, complex, tormented and strong medieval woman."[2] She was certainly troubled by male envy and domination but she claims that she was God's servant and God demanded her to write. She often shows herself as tormented but strong in her faith. Heinrich of Nördlingen, a fourteenth century priest describes her as a "true

---

[1] Grace M. Jantzen, *Power, Gender and Christian Mysticism*, p. 12.

[2] Susan Clark, "Introduction", *Flowing Light of Divinity*, p. xi.

friend of God" and a person "drawn up in the Spirit."[3] What mattered to her was the truth, the reality of union with God. She never allowed trivialities to distract her focus. What concerned her throughout her writings was her own experience of God. Even when things troubled her she did not turn to people for counsel or her own reason but always turned to God. However, she was not without external support from people who were persuaded by the authenticity of her spiritual experiences with God. Mechthild's spiritual adviser Heinrich of Halle, supported her, encouraged her and helped her to write down her thoughts and the nuns of Helfta protected and stood with her in her old age. Mechthild herself was not a passive victim of the powerful ecclesiastical hierarchy. No doubt Mechthild was aware of her femaleness. Like her, other women writers of her time were conscious of their inferior status as women and seemed to have accepted and lived with that awareness. For example, Hildegard of Bingen (1098-1179) refers to herself as a 'poor little creature.' Barbara Newman observes that Hildegard struggled with the gender difference. There was a tension in her mind between her gender and her position of authority. She struggled to overthrow male authorities and to set boundaries on the one hand and on the other to accept her inferior position in the male world. There was a conflict in her mind.[4]

In a similar manner, Mechthild's writing "shows a 'more anxious quality of writing' and seems more 'influenced by the contemporary stereotype of women as morally and

---

[3] Patricia Zimmerman Beckman, "The Power of Books and the Practice of Mysticism in the Fourteenth century: Heinrich of Nördlingen and Margaret Ebner on Mechthild's Flowing Light of the Godhead", p. 79.

[4] See, Barbara Newman, *Sisters of Wisdom: St Hildegard's Theology of the Feminine* (Berkeley: University of California Press, 1987), p. 35.

intellectually inferior.'"[5] In her dialogue with God, she expresses doubts about her right to speak. But "the more powerful, God's voice, the male voice, gives approval and encouragement to speak."[6] Likewise, at the beginning of the *Scivias*, Hildegard records that God's voice told that she has received her "profound insight not from humans, but from the lofty and tremendous Judge on high..."[7] And it was a heavenly command for her to say and write what she saw and heard.[8]

Her relationship with God was one of both submission and equality. She presents an idea of a loving God who relates to the devotee as an equal rather than as a patriarchal hierarchical authority. She knew God as lover and as the Supreme God; as the noble prince who embraces her, the little servant-girl that the two become one like water and wine.[9] In the loving relationship God becomes her equal.

It is this awareness of being both subject to God and being God's spouse that gives her the authority to record her immediate intimate experiences boldly and without any

---

[5] Caroline Walker Bynum, "Women Mystics in the Thirteenth Century: The Case of the Nuns of Helfta", in *Jesus as Mother: studies in the Spirituality of the High Middle Ages* (Berkeley: University of California Press, 1982), pp. 170-262, pp. 184-85, cited in Frank Tobin, *Mechthild von Magdeburg: A Medieval Mystic in Modern Eyes*, p. 123.

[6] Frank Tobin, *Mechthild von Magdeburg: A Medieval Mystic in Modern Eyes*, p. 104.

[7] Grace M. Jantzen, *Power, Gender and Christian Mysticism*, pp. 170-71, referring to Hildegard of Bingen, *Scivias*, translated by Columba Hart and Jane Bishop, Introduction by Barbara J. Newman, Classics of Western Spirituality Series (New York: Paulist, 1990), p. 59.

[8] Rosemary Radford Ruether, *Visionary Women: Three Medieval Mystics*, p. 8, citing "Declaration", *Scivias*, Hart and Bishop translation, p. 59.

[9] Book 1.4; Galvani, p. 9

inhibition. What comes through in her writings is the inner courage and conviction that she is called by God to record her experiences. Her authority was based on the knowledge of God she gained in the intimate relationship with God. Her knowledge of God enabled her to resist male power in order to own knowledge. She overturned the notion that only men received revelations and women played a secondary role in the church and in society. She tries to cross the set boundaries and invites her readers to reconsider women's role in Church and society.

Woman's Knowledge of God: An Embodied Knowledge

Mechthild's writing shows that there is a distinctive way of being, knowing and doing as a woman. Her self and voice develop in the intimate relationship of being a spouse of God. Her insights are gathered directly from her experiences. Thus, her knowledge is an embodied knowledge since her knowledge integrates feeling, passion and physical/biological knowing that does not negate intellect. Certainly, Mechthild's writings show a distinction between soul and body. She detests the body, sees it as a foe to the soul, calls the body a murderer and wants to be on guard against it.[10] She appraises the nobility of the soul. The soul turns toward all good things but the evil flesh is ignoble. The lust of human senses and the wishes of the flesh drive us away from God. God himself teaches the soul from "the depth of his heart" "constantly overflowing with goodness."[11]

Mechthild was writing in her own context. To a large extent she was the child of her own culture and thought patterns. She seems to accept unquestioningly the platonic dualistic notion

---

[10] Book 1.2; Galvani, pp. 6-8, p. 7. Also, Book 1.7; Galvani, p. 11; Book 1.10; Galvani, p. 11-12.

[11] Book 5. 22; Galvani, pp. 144-45, p. 145. Also, see Book 3. 21; Galvani, pp. 16-19.

which separated soul from the body and seems to work with the platonic assumption that the body is evil and the soul is good. This idea runs in major strands throughout the Christian West.[12] The detached intellect is exalted and the body is seen as a threat to the soul. Thus, Mechthild's writings show the dualist ideas of the distinction between soul and body. Yet, she is strongly focused on the body and sensuality. One can observe in her writing a great deal of emphasis on the body itself. In an interesting conversation between Love and the soul, the soul tells Love that she fasts, keeps vigils, is without mortal sin and that she is sufficiently bound. Love criticises the soul for concentrating more on body than on Jesus her sweet Lord.[13] However, she does not appear to revise the order of hierarchy of soul over the body. She seems to concentrate on both equally. vIn another conversation between God and the soul, God says to the soul,

'Dear dove, now hear Me:

My divine wisdom is so far above you

That I arrange My gifts in you in such a way

That your poor body can bear them.

Your secret search must find Me;

Your heart's misery must compel Me;

Your sweet pursuit tires Me so much

That I desire to cool Myself

in your pure soul

In which I am bound.

---

[12] See for medieval interest in Greek metaphysics, Colin Brown, *Philosophy and the Christian Faith: A Historical Sketch from the Middle Ages to the Present Day* (London: Tyndale Press, 1969), pp. 12-36.

[13] Book 2.23; Galvani, pp. 47-49, p. 47.

The throbbing of your sighing, wounded heart

Has driven My justice from you.

That is good for both of us.

I cannot be separated from you.

No matter how far apart we are,

We are not separated.

However lightly I caress you,

I inflict untold pain on your body.

If I were to give Myself to you at all times according to your
desire

I would deprive Myself of the sweet refuge

I have in you on earth.

For a thousand bodies

Could not contain the longing of a loving soul.'[14]

There is no flight from physicality. Physicality appears as the medium of religious experience. Love, longing and pain cannot be separated from emotional experiences. The spirituality of Mechthild is an affective spirituality that gives a place for love, desire and passions. In this sense, her knowledge of God is an embodied knowledge and it can be situated in the affective tradition of medieval age yet with a difference.

Jantzen in her book gives a detailed analysis of both the intellectual tradition and the affective tradition of knowing God.[15] The intellectual tradition is identified with Dionysius then with the major thinkers such as Albert the Great (c. 1200-

---

[14] Book 2.25, Galvani, pp. 52-55, p. 53.

[15] For a detailed study, refer to Grace M. Jantzen, Power, Gender and Christian Mysticism, pp. 108-122. Also refer to Sarah S. Poor, "Historicizing Canonicity: Tradition and the Invinsible Talent of Mechthild of Magdeburg ", pp. 49-72.

80), Thomas Aquinas (ca. 1225-1274) and later on with Meister Eckhart (1260-1328). The intellectual way of knowing centres on reason. For example, in Eckhart's writings, the progress of the soul is seen in terms of knowledge. He identifies man with reason and woman with sensuality. For Eckhart, genuine knowledge of God involves male reason and, therefore, women's sensory faculties and their visionary experiences could not be treated as spiritually significant.[16] The affective tradition of knowing God, of which Bernard of Clairvaux can be cited as a prime example, emphasises love but does not negate intellect. Reason and love enhance each other. For Bernard of Clairvaux love is fundamental to knowing God; the relationship between the soul and God centres in love. The divine empowers, elicits and raises the soul in love.[17] "Everything comes from and must lead to love"; "Out of love God seeks us and wants us to seek him. He longs for us, draws us to himself, and is present to us through his powerful words and in his Word."[18] The heart is the seat of knowing but the importance of mind is also emphasised. Love can bring healing in human personality that is distorted by sin. This moral transformation and healing by love can bring union with God who is caritas.[19]

Similar to Bernard of Clairvaux, Mechthild presents an affective way of knowing that emphasises love, passion, desire and longing to know God. In Mechthild's writings, love can be

---

[16] Grace M. Jantzen, *Power, Gender and Christian Mysticism*, pp. 118-120.

[17] Ray C. Petry, ed., *Late Medieval Mysticism* (London: SCM, 1957), p. 51.

[18] Jean Leclercq, "Introduction", *Bernard of Clairvaux: Selected Works*, translated and foreword G. R. Evans, Classics of Western Spirituality Series (New York and Mahwah, NI: Paulist Press, 1987), p. 32.

[19] Grace M. Jantzen, *Power, Gender and Christian Mysticism*, pp. 123 - 125. For a detailed study of affective tradition, Jantzen, *Power, Gender and Christian Mysticism*, pp. 123-131.

seen as a means of experiencing and uniting with God. The bridegroom and the bride share the same marriage-bed. They are united together in love. It is an ecstasy of a love fulfilled. "And in Bernard too, there is ecstasy, *ek stasis*, a standing outside of oneself; but it is as a broken vessel going completely into God, 'drunk with divine love', not an intellectual ecstasy that has passed into the unknowing beyond knowledge."[20] And "'the soul, drunk with divine love, forgetful of self, and seeming to be a broken vessel, goes completely into God, and cleaving to God becomes one spirit with him....'"[21]

Seen in this background of Intellectual and Affective ways of knowing God, it is clear that Mechthild's way of knowing forms a contrast to the intellectual way of knowing. In the affective tradition, which is not unlike intellectual tradition, spiritual love cannot be experienced if one is caught up in physical passion. For instance, although Bernard starts with an erotic language in his writings he soon tries to transpose it into a spiritual meaning. In other words, he substitutes actual bodily love with a language of passionate spirituality.[22] He works with the same Platonic assumption that human bodiliness and sexuality are a barrier to spiritual love. Further, when bodiliness and sexuality are linked with women the spiritual path is open to men alone. Hence, the affective tradition does not go very far from the intellectual tradition in this regard.

---

[20] Grace M. Jantzen, *Power, Gender and Christian Mysticism*, p. 125.

[21] Grace M. Jantzen, *Power, Gender and Christian Mysticism*, p. 125, citing Bernard of Clairvaux, *Treatises II*, (*The Steps of Humility, On Loving God*), Cistercian Fathers Series 13, Kalamazoo (Michigan: Cistercian Publications, 1974), p. 1.

[22] Grace M. Jantzen, *Power, Gender and Christian Mysticism*, pp. 128-29.

Mechthild goes beyond both the affective and intellectual trends in affirming the physical and sensory faculties of women.[23] Mechthild does not feel the need to put aside the things of the body. For her the body flows into the divine. Female images are found in her writings. For instance, in a dialogue between God and the soul, God says to the soul 'I am the light and your breast is the lantern.'[24] She speaks of Mary as a flower, a white lily, rose and noble queen.[25] She also speaks of her motherly countenance and motherly care.[26] She says, Mary's lovely breasts are brimming with sweet milk. Her milk flow on in honour of the heavenly father and for love of mankind.[27]

She sees Mary as a mediator who intercedes for the whole world and also a mother who suckles all the faithful people with the 'pure, unspoiled milk of true, tender mercy,' not only Christ and Christians, but also the prophets and sages before

---

[23] Carlos M. N. Eire in his review on *Meister Eckhart and the Beguine Mystics: Hadewijch of Brabant, Mechthild of Magdeburg and Marguerite Porete*, edited by Bernard McGinn, New York: Continuum, 1994, which is basically a collection of revised versions of the papers presented at the International Medieval Conference held in May 1993 states that the authors show parallels that exist between the writings of Meister Eckhart and the Beguines. Although it is not clear how Eckhart was influenced by beguine spirituality yet there are similarities especially concerning the ideas of the indwelling of divine presence and the process of self-emptying. See the review by Carlos M. N. Eire in *Church History*, 65, no. 3 (1996), pp. 467-68. Certainly, there are similarities between Eckhart's spirituality and the beguine spirituality, yet Mechthild's writings show characteristics that are unique and her religiosity is a type of her own.

[24] Book 3.12; Galvani, pp. 78-79.

[25] Book 7.19; Galvani, pp. 224-225.

[26] Book 7.20; Galvani, p. 225.

[27] Rosemary Radford Ruether, *Visionary Women: Three Medieval Mystics*, p. 32.

Christ was born, and Mary continues to do so until the day of Judgment.[28]

The maternal images that are used by Gertrude are very interesting. She speaks of God as a mother who teaches her daughter needle-work. God the mother tenderly and carefully holds the hands of the girl child and guides her to learn. God the mother seats the young little child who is naked, on her lap and covers the child with her own clothes, wraps the child and warms the child. But she is also a stern mother who disciplines her children. She even puts on terrifying masks and frightens her children so that they come running into her arms.[29]

Both Gertrude and Mechthild of Hackeborn use paternal and maternal images for God. In their writings the public and private roles interchange.For example, "'fathers feed and console, as do mothers; mothers teach, as do fathers: the full range of such images applies   both to God and to self. God is mother, emperor and pope; Mary is mother and queen; Mechthild herself is a prince leading an army, a preacher, a conduit for grace, a parent to her [spiritual] children.'"[30]

Marguerite of Oingt (died 1310) speaks of mother Jesus thus:

> My sweet Lord, I gave up for you my father and mother and my brothers and all the wealth of the world... For are you not my mother and more than my mother? The mother who

---

[28] Rosemary Radford Ruether, *Visionary Women: Three Medieval Mystics*, p. 37, referring to Galvani, pp. 15-16.

[29] Gertrude the Great of Helfta, *Gesandten der Gottlichen liebe*, trans. Walter Berschin, Heidelberg: Verlag Lambert Schneider, 1989, p. 445, cited in Grace M. Jantzen, *Power, Gender and Christian Mysticism*, pp. 298-99.

[30] Grace M. Jantzen, *Power, Gender and Christian Mysticism*, p. 229.

> bore me laboured in delivering me for one day or one night
> but you, my sweet and lovely Lord, laboured for me for more
> than thirty years. Oh, my sweet and lovely Lord, with what
> love you laboured for me and bore me through your whole
> life. But when the time approached for you to be delivered,
> your labour pains were so great that your holy sweat was
> like great drops of blood that came out from your body and
> fell on the earth...Ah! Sweet Lord Jesus Christ, who ever saw
> a mother suffer such a birth! For when the hour of your
> delivery came you were placed on the hard bed of cross...and
> your nerves and all your veins were broken. And truly it is
> no surprise that your veins burst when in one day you gave
> birth to the whole world.[31]

Julian makes a contrast between earthly mothers and the
mother Jesus.

> We know that all our mothers bear us for pain and for death.
> O, what is that? But our true Mother Jesus, he alone bears
> us for joy and for endless life, blessed may he be. So he carries
> us within him in love and travail, until the full time when he
> wanted to suffer the sharpest thorns and cruel pains that ever
> were or will be, and at last he died. And when he had finished,
> and had borne us for bliss, still all this could not satisfy his
> wonderful love....therefore he must needs nourish us, for the
> precious love of motherhood has made him our debtor.[32]

Thus, God is seen as mother and spoken of in female terms.
This validates the thought that mothering and femaleness can
be thought of as God-like. This gives rise to an embodied
knowledge of the image of God. The image of God resides in
the body. Jantzen comments "Had this line of thought been
carried forward, there would have been possible a significant
reclaiming of spirituality by and for women."[33]

---

[31] Caroline Walker Bynum, *Jesus as Mother: Studies in the Spirituality of
the High Middle Ages*, p. 153, cited in Grace M. Jantzen, *Power, Gender
and Christian Mysticism*, p. 300.

[32] Julian of Norwich, *Showings*, p. 298, cited in Grace M. Jantzen,
Power, Gender and Christian Mysticism, p. 302

[33] Grace M. Jantzen, *Power, Gender and Christian Mysticism*, pp. 303-4.

In Mechthild's writings, one of the dialogues between the Lord and the Lady soul reads as follows:

> Then the Most Beloved goes toward the Most Beautiful in the hidden chambers of the invisible Deity. There she finds the couch and the pleasure of Love, and God awaiting her in a superhuman fashion. This is what Our Lord says: - Stay, Lady Soul. – What is your wish, Lord? – That you should be naked. – Lord, how can this happen to me? – Lady Soul, you are so 'co-natured' in Me that nothing can be interposed between you and Me...your noble desire and your insatiable hunger ...I shall satisfy eternally with My infinite superabundance.[34]

This is a passionate encounter. The sexuality is explicit. Certainly it is a spiritual experience. Spiritual lessons are learned not by negating the passionate encounter but through such encounter and by affirming it.

Like Mechthild, Hadewijch expresses her passionate encounter with God explicitly. In the following vision that Hadewijch had in church she explains what happened to her.

> With that he came in the form and clothing of a Man, as he was on the day when he gave us his body for the first time; looking like a human being and a man, wonderful, and beautiful, and with glorious face, he came to me as humbly as anyone who wholly belongs to another. Then he gave himself to me in the shape of the sacrament...After that he came himself to me, took me entirely in his arms, and pressed me to him; and all my members felt his full felicity, in accordance with the desire of my heart and my humanity. So I was outwardly satisfied and fully transported...but soon, after a short time, I lost that manly beauty outwardly in the sight of his form...[35]

---

[34] Grace M. Jantzen, *Power, Gender and Christian Mysticism*, p. 133, citing, Emile Zum Brunn and Georgette Epiney-Burgard, *Women Mystics in Medieval Europe*, p. 59.

[35] Hadewijch, *The Complete Works*, p. 281, cited in Grace M. Jantzen, *Power, Gender and Christian Mysticism*, p. 135.

It is love-making and one can say that it is spiritual love-making. However, "it is not meant as an account of a physical occurrence which could have been observed by other people present in the church but neither is it meant as simply a figure of speech..."[36] Like Hadewijch, Julian of Norwich gives importance to the body. The physical and bodily reality is integrated into the spiritual. The body is cherished and has a part in spiritual progress; it is enfolded in the love of God.

The body is esteemed not merely because it sees the divine in material bodily reality but also because the body is a location of life itself, since all life occurs in body.[37] These women writers did not consider female sexuality as a hindrance to spiritual progress. They moved away from the then held common notion, that sin came into the world through a woman. Julian does not connect sin to women. Repentance is for the sin actually committed not for the sinfulness that is linked to Eve. Although Mechthild speaks about the sin committed by Eve and the loss of incorruptible bodies she says what was lost was recovered by Mary. For these women unnecessary guilt and shame is not the response that is appropriate to God. Spiritual progress involves self-knowledge but a differently constructed self-knowledge that takes women's own experiences seriously.

---

[36] Grace M. Jantzen, *Power, Gender and Christian Mysticism*, p. 135.

[37] Carol P. Christ, "Embodied, Embedded *Mysticism*, Affirming the Self and Others in a Radically Interdependent World", *Journal of Feminist Studies in Religion*, 24, no. 2 (2008), pp. 159-167, p. 164. Also see, Robert C. Fuller, "Faith of the Flesh: Bodily Sources of Spirituality", *Religious Studies Review*, 33, no. 4 (2007), 285-290. In this article, Robert C. Fuller, explains how George Lakeoff and Mark Johnson in *Philosophy in the Flesh* (New York: Basic books, 1999), draw the attention of the readers to the embodied nature of all thought. For him such thought proffers a religion from below.

Theology as a Reflection of Woman's Experience

In Medieval women writers in general there is not a systematic exposition of a spiritual path or steps to follow in spiritual progress. Their spiritual teachings are based on their own spiritual experiences. They based their authority on their visionary experiences. Mechthild, Hadewijch, Julian and others record their visions in their writings. Hildegard's *Scivias* ('*Know the Ways' of the Lord*), *The Book of Life's Merits* and *The Book of Divine Works* – are all three based on her visions. Gertrude of Helfta explains her salvific encounter with Christ dramatically and her authority was based on her visions that she received thereafter. She speaks of Christ as a young man whom she saw in her vision. She longed to be with him. But she saw a huge hedge of thorns between them. Then she says, "While I stood hesitating because of it, both burning with desire and almost fainting, he himself seized me swiftly and effortlessly, lifted me up, and set me beside him. But then I recognised on that hand...the glorious gems of those wounds which cancelled the debts of all."[38] The intimate relationship and union with God enabled them to have the inner vision of God. Gertrude, in another vision, speaks of receiving eucharist from Christ himself when she was in her sickbed and was unable to attend the eucharist.[39] Women's self understanding and their understanding of God grew as they experienced the visions. They became spiritual instructors to others.

---

[38] Gertrude the Great of Helfta, *The Herald of God's Loving Kindness*, Books 1 & 2, translated and annotated by Alexandra Barratt, Cistercian Fathers Series, 35 (Kalamazoo, Michigan: Cistercian Publications, 1991), p. 100, cited in Grace M. Jantzen, *Power, Gender and Christian Mysticism*, p. 164.

[39] Grace M. Jantzen, *Power, Gender and Christian Mysticism*, p. 211.

What we read in Mechthild's book is her own spiritual experiences. Woman's experience is a key to interpret Mechthild's writings. She bears witness to God's activity in her life. There is a mixture of prose and verse in her writings which are empowered by her experiences of God. Mechthild claims that "she is God's instrument, a means by which he communicates with humankind."[40] From the time of Plato, it is commonplace to think that men belonged to the realm of mind, reason and public life and that women belonged to the realm of emotion, body and private life. Spirituality in the early Christian times was seen in the spirit or intellect or mind. Mechthild, on the contrary, attempted to understand God through her inner senses, an immediate knowledge of God occurs in the intimate relationship with God. This says something about human knowing as well as divine knowing. From the human point of view, to know God is to be known by God. Mechthild, like Plato seems to think that true knowledge occurs when the knower and the known are united. Also, Dionysius, concerning God's understanding, reckons that "God knows all things, not by understanding things, but by understanding himself."[41] Hence, it is possible to say that God understands or knows humans in the intimate relationship by knowing himself. Mechthild's spiritual experiences, her way of knowing God and being known by God is not far from a Platonic and Dionysian line of thought yet Mechthild differs from the intellectual tradition of both Plato and Dionysius. For them knowing occurs only in the mind and is seen as a male prerogative. In Plato's *Phaedrus* the lover and the beloved, are

---

[40] Frank Tobin, *Mechthild von Magdeburg: A Medieval Mystic in Modern Eyes*, p. ix.

[41] Grace M. Jantzen, *Power, Gender and Christian Mysticism*, p. 104, citing Pseudo-Dionysius, *The Complete Writings*, translated by Colm Luibheid and Paul Rorem, Classics of Western Spirituality (New York: Paulist, and London: SPCK), p. 108.

both male and there is no place for woman here. The erotic attraction between the two men "is not consummated physically, but instead the physical desire is channelled toward spiritual consummation, the union of their minds."[42]

In Mechthild's writing, the soul is a female and the lover, God, is the male Beloved. The love relationship is between male and female. It is heterosexual rather than homosexual. In Hadewijch's writing, the soul is portrayed as the knight. The soul is male and God is the Lady Love. The following poem speaks about the relationship between God the female and the soul, the male.

> He who serves Love has a hard adventure
>
> Before he knows Love's mode of action,
>
> Before he is fully loved by her.
>
> He tastes her as bitter and sour;
>
> He cannot rest for an instant,
>
> So long as Love does not fetter him completely in love
>
> And bring him into the union of fruition.[43]

Moreover, Hadewijch, when speaking about 'fruition of love', uses the metaphors of food and eating. Her passionate encounter with God involves her whole being, not merely the union of spirit or mind.[44] In the following poem she speaks about eating, drinking and the consummation of love.[45]

---

[42] Grace M. Jantzen, *Power, Gender and Christian Mysticism*, p. 36.

[43] Hadewijch, *The Complete Works*, p. 131, cited in Grace M. Jantzen, *Power, Gender and Christian Mysticism*, p. 136.

[44] Grace M. Jantzen, *Power, Gender and Christian Mysticism*, pp. 136-137.

[45] For more on eating, fasting and spirituality of women see, Caroline Walker Bynum, *Holy Feast and Holy Fast: The Religious Significance of Food to Medieval Women* (Berkeley: California University Press, 1987).

So for the soul things go marvellously;

While desire pours out and pleasure drinks,

The soul consumes what belongs to it in love

And sinks with frenzy into Love's fruition.

So in love the loving soul has full success,

When Love with love fully gives her love;

Thus is the loving soul well fed by Love alone,

Where it enjoys sweet Love.[46]

In Mechthild's writings, as mentioned earlier, the lady soul is embraced and kissed by God the Beloved. In this close proximity knowledge of God occurs. These women seem to think holistically for their experiences involve passions and emotions but not without the involvement of the mind; understanding and tasting, reasoning and passionate love-making are seen in harmony. Often religious women were said to fast since they controlled the consumption of their food to the extent of starvation. But often their fasting and feasting go together. Mechthild presents a vision of feasting on the eucharist.

In one of her visions, John the Baptist came to be her celebrant when she was unable to attend the mass.

Then the maid [Mechthild] went up to the altar with great love and widely opened soul. John the Baptist took the white lamb with the red wounds and laid it on the mouth of the maid. Thus the pure lamb laid itself on its own image in the stall of her body and sucked her heart with its tender lips.[47]

---

[46] Hadewijch, *The Complete Works*, p. 244, cited in Grace M. Jantzen, *Power, Gender and Christian Mysticism*, p. 136.

[47] Mechthild of Magdeburg, *The Revelations of Mechthild of Magdeburg (1210-1297) or The Flowing Light of the Godhead*, translated by Lucy Menzies (London: Longmans, Green and Co., 1953), p. 133, cited in Grace M. Jantzen, *Power, Gender and Christian Mysticism*, p. 211.

We have here the image of feasting on the eucharist. It is the image of "eating and being eaten, nursing and being nursed: the blood of Christ is the essential spiritual sustenance ..."[48]

Mechthild's speech emerges from this experience that she had with God. Hermann Kunisch says that Mechthild has to speak "because her heart is so full."[49] According to Ulrich Müller, Mechthild's writing can be considered a 'reflective autobiography' since it reflects her insights and experiences. It has "qualities of a testimonial."[50] Tobin remarks that "her writing is doxology, spontaneous praise of God corresponding to the spontaneous and overpowering grace bestowed upon her."[51] Hence, it is possible to say that Mechthild contributes to the aspect of theology of immediate experience of God. Her theology is a pure reflection on her own experience. Thus, women, understanding God through experience, attain a prime place in the history of Christian theology. Further, it calls for an epistemological modesty formed in the recognition that male's judgement and voices need to be tested by listening to other voices that are previously excluded or ignored. They also call for an epistemological privilege for women's voice since their voices and woman's way of knowing were not taken into serious consideration and still are not heard as they should be heard.

---

[48] Grace M. Jantzen, *Power, Gender and Christian Mysticism*, p. 211.

[49] Hermann Kunisch, "Die mittelalterliche Mystik und die deutsche Sprache", in his *Kleine Schriften* (Berlin: Kuncker und Humblot, 1968), pp. 21-78, pp. 53-55, cited in Frank Tobin, *Mechthild von Magdeburg: A Medieval Mystic in Modern Eyes*, p. 77.

[50] Ulrich Müller, "Mechthild von Magdeburg und Dantes Vita Nuova oder erotische Religiosität und religiöse Erotik," in *Liebe als Literatur: Aufsätze zur erotischen Dichtug in Deutschland*, Ed. Rüdiger Krohn, Munich, 1983, pp. 163-76, pp. 164-66, cited in Frank Tobin, *Mechthild von Magdeburg: A Medieval Mystic in Modern Eyes*, p. 89.

[51] Frank Tobin, *Mechthild von Magdeburg: A Medieval Mystic in Modern Eyes*, p. 68.

Love and Alienation: Two Forms of Woman's Devotion

Mechthild proffers two forms of devotion: one is the intense love between God and the soul, which results in union. The other is the painful experience of alienation or abandonment or separation from God, which results in more love for God. Very splendidly, Mechthild's writings present the readers with the beautiful theme of mutual love between the lover and the beloved. She personally experienced joy and bliss of love. She also experienced the alienation of God. She knew the depth of God's love and the depth of pain of being alienated from God. She maintains in her writings that suffering and abandonment by God are necessary for growth since love intensifies after abandonment by the beloved. In the absence of God, the soul recollects the experience of blissful union with God, God's lust, desire and longing for the soul. The soul suffers because of the desire she has for the absent lover. For Mechthild, experiencing alienation from God is like living in the true desert.

This kind of experience is not exclusive to women writers but it is also expressed in male writers in the form of longing love for God. In Bernard of Clairvaux, the love of the bridegroom to his love and his absence and the ensuing pain the bride experiences are elaborated.

> The Bride pines away with love and is in cruel torment; having enjoyed union with the Beloved, she now finds it more painful to be separated from him. The Bridegroom's slowness to return is a bitter affliction to the Bride and his absence only heightens both her desire and her sorrow. However he may hurry to ease her impatience, she is consumed with longing until he returns.[52]

In Bernard's view, Jesus comes, loves but also withdraws in order to win our love and that we may love him even more. For Diego De Estella (1524-1578), a Spanish writer, love and

---

[52] Leclercq, "Introduction", *Bernard of Clairvaux: Selected Works*, p. 47.

desire are immeasurable, the tears of longing cannot be expressed by words. The soul is tortured by inward thirst like the hart pants for water.[53] Luis De Granada (1504-1588), another Spanish writer, begs the Lord not to flee away from him because he is for the Lord and the Lord is for him. The Lord is his final goal and he will reach him by all means even if he has to make a way through steel and fire. God is his well-being and final goal. His love for God is so intense that he can never ever stop loving the Lord. Such love is called unitive because its nature is to unite the lover with the beloved. There is no repose or rest apart from God because his heart is set on God alone who is his crown of all the desires, the final goal in life. He cries saying, "Although weary, slow are my steps, I turn back often, halt on the way yet please wait for me."[54]

The knowledge of God happens in the longing love for God. God hurts, wounds, pierces. The soul throbs with pain and waits for the healing, waits for God that he may illumine her. The soul comes to the knowledge within that "Only in the state of Union can true rest be found: till then, all is energy, activity, strife."[55]

In Mechthild's presentation, the youthful Christ who entices the soul is also the sufferer. Hence, the soul that loves Christ also participates in physical suffering. In book 1.29, she brings together these two themes: enjoyment and persecution. The youthful Christ entices the soul saying:

'See how beautiful My eyes are,

how right My mouth is,

how fiery My heart is,

how agile My hands are,

---

[53] E. Allison Peers, *Spanish Mysticism: A Preliminary Survey*, p. 145.
[54] *Ibid.*, p. 96.
[55] *Ibid.*, p. 44.

how quick My feet are,

and follow Me.

You shall be martyred with Me,

betrayed by envy,

sought out by falsehood,

captured by hatred,

bound by slander,

blindfolded so that the truth may be withheld from you,

slapped by the wrath of the world,

brought before the court in confession,

boxed on the ears with punishment,

sent before Herod in scorn,

undressed in wretchedness,

flogged with poverty,

crowned by temptation,

looked down upon in degradation;

you shall bear your cross despising sin,

shall be crucified renouncing all that you desire,

be nailed to the cross with holy virtues;

wounded by love,

you shall die on the cross with holy constancy,

be pierced in your heart by constant union,

removed from the cross in true victory over all your foes,

buried in obscurity,

and, finally, in a holy conclusion,

you shall rise from the dead and ascend into heaven,

drawn in by God's breath.'[56]

---

[56] Galvani, p. 18.

Love and pain, enjoyment and suffering, union and separation are woven so beautifully. As Ulrike Wiethaus says Mechthild's presentation offers a new interpretation of Christ's suffering itself and thereby it has much to say about human existence, love, pain and following Christ. Wiethaus writes,

> this stark juxtaposition of youthful beauty and its enjoyment and the brutality of physical persecution reinforces the theological meaning of Christ's crucifixion in an unexpected way. It increases the sympathy and compassion of the onlooker who meditatively identifies with Christ, and underlines the heroism of self-sacrifice. But it also teaches the coincidence of paradoxical truths: pleasure as well as pain demarcate human existence in the experience of ultimate reality. In the experiential Minnemystik of the beguines, Christ becomes the siren whose attractiveness lures the spiritual traveller into an experience of death, and promises rebirth.[57]

Re-living Christ's Passion and Suffering

Mechthild's Christ-centered spirituality sees suffering as a way of knowing Christ and reaching Christ. Mechthild and other women such as Julian identified with the human suffering of Christ by their sickness. Their self-inflicted suffering is a way of knowing Christ. By suffering in order to know Christ, they gave themselves for the redemption of the world.

Julian of Norwich prayed for a 'recollection of the passion.' She wished to participate in the suffering and death of Jesus rather than being a detached observer. And she did receive such vision when she fell ill and lay in her sick bed. All the people standing around her thought that she was going to die. The parson was called for and he came with a crucifix and

---

[57] Ulrike Wiethaus, "Sexuality, Gender, and the Body in Late Medieval Women's Spirituality: Cases from Germany and Netherlands", *Journal of Feminist Studies in Religion*, 7, no.1 (1991), 35-52, p. 44.

asked her to fix her eyes on the crucifix she suddenly saw blood streaming from it.[58]

Bynum says that religious women of this age celebrated the religious possibilities of their bodiliness.

> Medieval women are not best understood as creatures constrained and impelled by society's notions of the female as inferior. Women's piety was not, fundamentally, internalized dualism or misogyny...In their symbols women expanded the suffering, giving self they were ascribed by their culture, becoming ever more wonderfully and horribly the body on the cross. They became that body not as a flight from but as a continuation of the self. And...that body was also God.[59]

Mechthild concentrates a great deal on the suffering body which for her reflects divinity since "pain manifests a reality that is contained in divinity." Hence it can be said that "suffering body is also the divine body"[60] Mechthild shows in her writing how body's worth is expressed in Christ and Mary. Christ gives birth to the soul through his wounds and Mary suckles each soul and the whole of Christianity until it grows to maturity.[61] This is a theology of body which takes into account pain and sufferings and the way towards union with God through suffering.

Sarah Hopper in her book, *Mothers, Mystics and Merrymakers* gives a detailed analysis of women pilgrims who undertook pilgrimage for their passionate love of Christ. Women pilgrims

---

[58] Grace M. Jantzen, *Power, Gender and Christian Mysticism*, pp. 166-67.

[59] Caroline Walker Bynum, *Jesus as Mother: Studies in the Spirituality of the High Middle Ages*, p. 295, cited in Grace M. Jantzen, *Power, Gender and Christian Mysticism*, p. 215.

[60] Michelle Voss Roberts, "Flowing and Crossing: The Somatic Theologies of Mechthild and Lalleśwari", *Journal of the American Academy of Religion*, p. 659.

[61] *Ibid.*, p. 657.

re-lived the passion of Christ as they travelled around the Holy Land and the Holy Sepulchre in Jerusalem. Their mystical perception, or seeing with the eyes of their soul, could associate the physical with the spiritual state.[62] This is a powerful experience.

Women's bodily sufferings such as fasting, control of sex – being virgins, flagellations of the body, requesting God to offer them pain, illness and suffering are the ways to reach God. Seeing with the eyes of their souls, re-living the past as they journeyed through various places in the Holyland, remembering, recollecting biblical accounts of Christ's birth and, as they entered the holy tomb remembering his death, are all ways of knowing God.[63] Their emotional responses and outpourings when they visited those places form a narrative theology.

Woman's Spirituality: An Integration of Public and Private
In Mechthild's life and writing, public, social and spiritual or inner subjective relation of the soul to God were not set in opposites. The inner potential of her experience has transformatory power and lends itself to communion and friendship. Mechthild shows how being in relationship with God at a personal level can become a source of relationship with others in the human community. For her, the service to humanity is a path of love and Christian spirituality.

---

[62] Sarah Hooper, *Mothers, Mystics and Merrymakers* (Gloucestershire: Sutton Publishing Ltd., 2006), p. 22.

[63] Mary Solberg proposes another aspect of knowing, namely, epistemology of compelling knowledge of the Cross, where the knowledge of the Cross compels a commitment. It is a lived experience; seeing, knowing and doing from the perspective of victims. See, Mary Solberg, *Compelling Knowledge: A Feminist Proposal for an Epistemology of the Cross* (Albany: State University of New York, 1997).

For the medieval religious women in general, spirituality involves sharing the sufferings of Christ. Embracing Christ or to be embraced by him means embracing Christ's humanity and thereby Christ's sufferings. It is pouring one's life in service to others. Only by including this aspect of kenosis, giving oneself to others, could their spirituality become meaningful and authentic. In early Christianity, for example in Origen and Dionysius and in the medieval era in Meister Eckhart's writing, the union with God is seen as the ultimate goal and there is no indication of going beyond and living out this experience in society. But with the religious women of the medieval age it is not the case. For example, God says to Hadewijch, 'Go forth and live what I am.' For Hadewijch the 'fruition of love' or 'to be God with God' as Jantzen comments, "involves an identification with the humanity and divinity of Christ, sharing concretely in his self-sacrificing care for those who needed him, in the way that the beguine communities were putting into practice throughout northern Europe. This was the way in which Hadewijch believed that she for whom Christ had become human could with him become God."[64]

She instructs the young Beguines that performing acts of love is a way to be wholly united with God.[65] She teaches them "to seek after nothing but Love, work nothing but Love, protect nothing but Love, and advance nothing but Love."[66] Jantzen comments, "These can be no idle words from a beguine, committed as they were to the service of the sick and distressed at a time when social services were urgently needed and in short supply, and when they were likely as not to be persecuted

---

[64] Grace M. Jantzen, *Power, Gender and Christian Mysticism*, p. 140.

[65] *Ibid.*, p. 142.

[66] Hadewijch, *The Complete Works*, p. 84, cited in Grace M. Jantzen, *Power, Gender and Christian Mysticism*, p. 142.

for their pains."[67] Although, religious women were held in suspicion by the male hierarchy, religious women in general assisted the clergy by their spiritual activities in many ways. Bynum notes that as the Church was led by male clergies, religious women supported the clergy by their piety and by functioning as counsellors, mediators and channels to the sacraments. Their spirituality aided and supported the clergy rather than undermining the clergy.[68] However, some instances reveal that women claimed equal authority in the church or in the institutions. Mechthild for example, in her old age at Helfta invited the young members of the convent to receive eucharist from her hands.

> Yet I, least of all souls,
>
> Take him in my hand
>
> Eat him and drink him,
>
> And do with him what I will!
>
> Why then should I trouble myself
>
> As to what the angels experience?[69]

In one of her visions, she receives the eucharist from "John the Baptist, a lay-man not a priest."[70]

---

[67] Grace M. Jantzen, *Power, Gender and Christian Mysticism*, p. 143.

[68] Frank Tobin, *Mechthild von Magdeburg: A Medieval Mystic in Modern Eyes*, p. 123, referring to Caroline Walker Bynum, "Women Mystics in the Thirteenth Century: The Case of the Nuns of Helfta", in *Jesus as Mother: studies in the Spirituality of the High Middle Ages*, pp. 170-262, pp. 184-85.

[69] Mechthild of Magdeburg, *The Revelations of Mechthild of Magdeburg (1210-1297) or The Flowing Light of the Godhead*, p. 174, cited in Grace M. Jantzen, *Power, Gender and Christian Mysticism*, p.174.

[70] Sarah S. Poor, "Mechthild von Magdeburg, Gender, and the 'Unlearned Tongue'", *Journal of Medieval and Early Modern Studies*, p. 227.

It may very well lead one to wonder whether she was attempting to alter gender roles in the church or institution. Or it could mean that she affirms that she is exercising her teaching role and service within the context of the church authority and teaching. As Sarah S. Poor says Mechthild defends orthodoxy "in the face of a debased secular clergy that ignores it."[71] Whatever may be, it seems clear that medieval religious women's intimate loving relationship with God, their visionary experiences, their self-understanding as spouses of God, their identification with the sufferings of Christ – all gave them an authority that is an alternative to the established authority of ecclesiastical office. They challenge the readers to view leadership from a different perspective.

Furthermore, these women were meaningfully involved in public life. Hildegard served as abbess, Gertrude held spiritual leadership at Helfta, Hadewijch instructed the young Beguines, Bridget of Sweden and Teresa of Avila were involved in reforming their convents. These women confronted bishops and prelates, popes and kings when they acted wrongly and unjustly. They did so on the basis of their visionary experience; a direct vision from God. This was the authority for their teaching role and leadership.[72]

They also derived their authority by imitating or modelling themselves on Mary (*imitatio Marie*). We have already mentioned Hildegard's reference to herself as 'a poor little figure of a woman.' Jantzen says this kind of self-abasement or 'modesty formula' was apparently obligatory for medieval women writers but Hildegard, by referring to herself in this

---

[71] Sarah S. Poor, *Mechthild of Magdeburg and Her Book: Gender in the Making of Textual Authority* (Philadelphia: University of Pennsylvania Press, 2004), p. 48.

[72] Grace M. Jantzen, *Power, Gender and Christian Mysticism*, p. 169.

manner, compares herself to Mary the mother of Christ. Mary referred to herself as the humble handmaid of God. Her humility offered her the most exalted status of being the mother of Christ. Imitating Mary's humility means that women gain the privilege of receiving God's favour and spiritual authority.[73] The more humble they are the more receptive they become to God.

Some women emulated Mary in their everyday life. It is said of Bridget of Sweden (b. 1303-1373) that she experienced a mystical pregnancy that "she could sense the quickening of a baby inside her – Bridget's symbolic manifestation of the entry of Christ into her heart. She also claimed that the Virgin appeared to her on Christmas Day to reassure her that what she had experienced was a re-creation of the Virgin's own joy at the divine conception and birth of the Christ child."[74] Hooper says that this experience enabled Bridget to think of herself "the earthly ambassador and instrument of revelation of Christ and the Virgin and the medium through which they would impart their wisdom and counsel as to the ways in which she could improve the spiritual observance of the world."[75]

It is often considered that the spirituality of inner subjective relation of the soul to God is an essentially private, subjective matter which does not connect with issues of social justice. Social justice belongs to the public realm. It is men's realm and men took those issues seriously. Further, "it is also deemed

---

[73] *Ibid.*, p. 170. For a different perspective of humility and authority in medieval religious women see Amy Hollywood, "'Who Does She Think She Is?': Christian Women's Mysticism", *Theology Today*, 60 (2003), 5-15. Hollywood argues that the religious women were not narcissistic rather their authority was based on the paradoxical interplay of humility and the claim of being chosen by God to mediate God's word to the world.

[74] Sarah Hooper, *Mothers, Mystics and Merrymakers*, p. 116.

[75] *Ibid.*

that women are 'naturally' more spiritual than men, then only a small step is necessary to confine both the 'feminine' and the 'spiritual' to a context in which they are rendered thoroughly ineffectual."[76] But Mechthild and other medieval religious women prove it wrong. We have shown in the section 'knowing in Mission' how Mechthild sees herself as a mediator between humans and divine. In her life and works, she brings spirituality and social justice, religion and politics together. There is a narration of personal and social responsibilities in her writings. These women led a way to a 'new mysticism'[77] which sought to see a relationship between world and the mendicant life, between men and women and between clergy and laity. Mechthild's mystic way does not confine her to a private realm but rather she becomes an instrument of integrating private and public.This statement leads us to examine whether Mechthild was a mystic and, if so, what are the special features of her mysticism?

Mechthild, a Beguinemystic

There are a number of theologians who argue that Mechthild was a Beguinemystic. Ursula Peters thinks Mechthild's writing can be considered as reflecting chief aspects of Beguinemystik. It reflects "concerns specific to the way of life of beguines." Peters notes that Mechthild's writing demonstrates her insecurity, that it reflects how she was opposed by the male clergy and how she reacted to their attacks. It also reflects her voluntary departure from her home and loved ones, her

---

[76] Grace M. Jantzen, *Power, Gender and Christian Mysticism*, pp. 17-18.

[77] Bernard McGinn shows how women's spirituality at this time was different from men's spirituality that called for a withdrawal from the world. For example, Bernard of Clairvaux's message of union with God called for a life of seclusion from the world. See, Bernard McGinn, "The Changing Shape of Late Medieval Mysticism", *Church History*, 65, no.2 (1996), 197-219, p. 198.

troubles or the troubles Beguines faced, her illness and her decision to enter the convent at Helfta. She led a holy life cultivating charity, humility, patience and meekness.[78] As Peters thinks, it is certain that Mechthild was shaped by the Beguine way of life and freedom. Beguines had intellectual independence although they received spiritual direction from Franciscans or Dominicans. Mechthild used her intellectual independence. This comes across in her writings and they show that she was shaped by the Beguine community and way of life. Grete Luers thinks that she must also have had spiritual inputs from the opportunities that she had had to converse privately with a well-educated confessor, she must have had opportunities to listen to sermons, and further the regular religious instructions she received, and her own contemplation and meditative prayer would have shaped her spirituality. [79]

Peter Gall Morel suggests that the origins of Mechthild's thought were to be found in her visions, outpourings of feelings and fantasy. However, he does not deny that Mechthild's writings lacked any intellectual content. He thinks that in Mechthild's writing there is a balance of the four elements that are necessary for a true member of a Beguine community namely "rational knowledge, vision of fantasy, enjoyment of feeling and immediacy of a higher state."[80]

Thus, a number of scholars argue that Mechthild is a Beguinemystic. But the most fundamental question is: 'Would

---

[78] Frank Tobin, *Mechthild von Magdeburg: A Medieval Mystic in Modern Eyes*, pp. 128 -129, citing Ursula Peters, *Religiöse Erfahrung als literarisches Faktum: Zur Vorgeschichte und Genese frauenmystischer Texte des 13 und 14, Jahrhundrets* (Tübingen: Max Niemeyer, 1988).

[79] Frank Tobin, *Mechthild von Magdeburg: A Medieval Mystic in Modern Eyes*, p. 43.

[80] Peter Gall Morel, "Vorrede und Einleitung", 1989, p. xxxii, cited in Frank Tobin, *Mechthild von Magdeburg: A Medieval Mystic in Modern Eyes*, p. 25.

Mechthild prefer to call herself a mystic?' Tobin thinks that Mechthild would not prefer to be called a mystic since "in her time the word existed only as an adjective that was never used to describe a person. It usually referred to one manner of interpreting scripture."[81]

The term mysticism comes from the Greek term *mustikos*, which in turn can be derived from the verb *mus*, meaning 'I close my eyes.' In ancient Greek thought the mystics were the people who had "devoted themselves to the mystery religions and had been initiated into their secret rituals." Hence, the phrase 'I close my eyes' refers to those who have closed their mouths or "kept silence and did not reveal the secrets of their initiation and the rituals through which the initiation was accomplished."[82] In the understanding of the later Christian platonists, the idea of what is mystical is moved from the meaning of the closing of the senses to cleansing of all desires and striving toward the Ultimate.[83]

Dionysius saw mystical and mysterious as almost synonymous. The term *mustikos* referred to "the secret initiation rites of the ancient meaning of scripture, and extended it to the sacraments, to the organisation of the church, and to theology itself."[84] Meister Eckhart's definition of the term focuses on the identity of being. Eckhart saw the antic foundation of the self or soul as the divine spark that is found within the soul or self. Human beings are aware of this ineffability of the absolute divine mystery. Hence, mysticism refers to the participation of human spirit in the Divine or the

---

[81] Frank Tobin, *Mechthild von Magdeburg: A Medieval Mystic in Modern Eyes*, p. ix.

[82] Grace M. Jantzen, *Power, Gender and Christian Mysticism*, p. 27.

[83] *Ibid.*, p. 34.

[84] Grace M. Jantzen, *Power, Gender and Christian Mysticism*, p. 96.

Absolute.[85] For Bernard of Clairvaux what is mystical is not confined to the meaning of scripture or to the intellectual progress; it is extended to experience. For him, mystical means experience.[86]

Contemporary definitions of mysticism abound. Numerous ways of understanding mysticism make it difficult to define. Certain mystics have described mysticism as union with God. Bernard McGinn describes mysticism as "a part or element of religion; mysticism as a process or way of life; and mysticism as an attempt to express a direct consciousness of the presence of God."[87] According to William James, mystical experience involves ineffability, noetic quality, transiency and passivity.[88] Underhill defines mysticism as "an active life-process of the 'whole self', aimed at the 'changeless One', which is a loving and personal object of love, culminating in union with the One in a 'unitive' state."[89] According to the *Catholic Encyclopedia*, mysticism is "a religious tendency and desire of the human soul towards an intimate union with the Divinity through contemplation and love. This contemplation...is not based on a merely analogical knowledge of the Infinite, but [is] a direct and immediate intuition of the infinite."[90] Robert Elwood defines mystical experience as "Experience in a religious

---

[85] Frank Tobin, *Mechthild von Magdeburg: A Medieval Mystic in Modern Eyes*, p. 111.

[86] Grace M. Jantzen, *Power, Gender and Christian Mysticism*, p. 126.

[87] Bernard McGinn, *Foundations of Mysticism* (New York: Crossroad, 1991), p. xv.

[88] William James, *The Varieties of Religious Experience*, The Gifford Lectures of 1901-2 (Glasgow: Collins, 1960), p. 367.

[89] Evelyn Underhill, *Mysticism: A Study in the Nature and Development of Man's Spiritual Consciousness* (London: Methuen, 1945), p. 81.

[90] See, Jerome Gellman, *Mystical Experience of God: A Philosophical Inquiry*, p.4.

context that is immediately or subsequently interpreted by the experience as a direct, unmediated encounter with ultimate divine reality. This experience engenders a deep sense of unity and suggests that during the experience, the experience was living on a level of being other than the ordinary."[91]

In light of these definitions, I prefer to state simply that Mechthild, like Bernard, speaks about experiential knowing and particularly woman's way of knowing God. She does speak about cleansing of the desires like Christian platonists. Her experience is a direct and immediate intuition of the divine. Her object of love was God and she had a direct consciousness of the presence of God. Mechthild understood God deep within herself as the ground of her own being. She presents a mystic experience of deep awareness of God within. It is based on experience and not a conceptual knowledge or theoretical knowledge. It is an inner subjective relation of the soul to God. It is subjective but an authentic subjective experience which contains within itself a true objectivity. Mechthild's mysticism centres on heart and love. However, she does not despise reason. Passionate erotic love is not suppressed rather spiritual wholes occur in such love, thus integrating physical into spirituality. Her construction of mysticism and her understanding of spirituality are quite different from that of the male writers of her time. Her authority was based on her visionary experiences.

Her mysticism concerns being and becoming. Luce Irigary says, "God forces us to do nothing except *become*. The only task, the obligation laid upon us is: to become divine men and women, to become perfect, to refuse to allow parts of ourselves

---

[91] *Ibid.* For definitions of mysticism refer also to Daniel E. Wigner, "Clarity in the Midst of Confusion: Defining Mysticism", *Perspectives in Religious Studies*, 34, no. 3 (2007), 331-345.

to shrivel and die that have the potential for growth and fulfilment."[92] Likewise, in her work *Becoming Divine*, Grace Jantzen centres on 'becoming divine' through 'natality' or the continued coming to birth of the self."[93]

Jantzen argues in her book, that defining mysticism as ineffability confines the discussion to the realm of emotions and thus removes it from reason, the public world and the world of men. This marginalises women and confines them to a private realm thus removing them from the political world and men's world.[94] But Mechthild, as we have discussed above, saw herself as a mediator between private and public life. Having looked at the term mysticism in the context of Mechthild's own experiences we now come back to the question of whether or not Mechthild was a Beguinemystic.

It seems plausible that Mechthild can be considered a Beguine mystic since she does show the characteristics and experiences that are unique to Beguine community. However, a close observation of Mechthild's writings shows two things clearly: firstly, her independence in her writing although she belonged to a community. She is aware of her lack of formal education. She shows certain freedom in her writings, which comes from her immediate experience with God alone. Secondly, the mixing of emotional element and intellectual element in her writings in a way that is different from other medieval writers.

Here again, a number of theologians agree about Mechthild's independence in her writing. For example, Hans

---

[92] Luce Irigary, *Sexes and Genealogies* (New York and Chichester: Columbia University Press, 1993), pp. 68-9.

[93] Grace M. Jantzen, *Becoming Divine: Towards a Feminist Philosophy of Religion* (Manchester: Manchester University Press, 1998), p. 117.

[94] Jerome Gellman, *Mystical Experience of God: A Philosophical Inquiry*, pp. 105ff.

Newman compares Mechthild's writing with other Beguines and proves her independence in her writings. Mechthild wrote her thought and experiences in her mother tongue. Hadewijch also expressed her thoughts in her mother tongue. Neumann thinks that it was likely that Mechthild was familiar with Hadewijch's writings.[95] Both Mechthild and Hadewijch use poetry to express. It is simple, beautiful, intimate and personal. Both use courtly style to express spiritual love. Perhaps they have used the same sources such as Song of Songs, Gospel of John, Apocalypse, Bernard of Clairvaux, Richard of St. Victor, Psuedo-Dionysius. Newmann also finds similarities in the mixing of these elements.[96]

However Neumann stresses Mechthild's independence. There are differences between Hadewijch and Mechthild in terms of poetic forms and even differences in their personalities and their conceptions of poetic forms. She was not influenced by Hadewijch and there was no Dutch influence. Neumann writes,

> If she remained all in all completely herself and gave more importance to what she saw inwardly than to what of literature she assimilated and to what she pondered, if her poetic temperament found expression more in the simple basic forms of religious and secular lyric poetry than in the complicated verse structures of courtly strophe, then this bears witness to the intellectual independence of this Magdeburg beguine who retained the power to adapt all these various impulses for her own possibilities of expression.[97]

---

[95] Frank Tobin, *Mechthild von Magdeburg: A Medieval Mystic in Modern Eyes*, p. 71.

[96] *Ibid.*, p. 72.

[97] Hans Neumann, "Der Minne Spiegel und Mechthild von Magdeburg", *Zeitschrift für deutsche Philologie*, 73 (1954), 217-26, p. 244, cited in Frank Tobin, *Mechthild von Magdeburg: A Medieval Mystic in Modern Eyes*, p. 72.

Likewise, Caroline Walker Bynum thinks that although she was a beguine and lived in that community she speaks of herself as an individual who is alone with God.[98]

With regard to the affective and intellectual elements in her writings, Friedrich-Wilhelm Wentzlaff-Eggbert thinks Mechthild's mysticism does not centre on personal and inner experiences since Mechthild's feeling and passion are balanced by the way she uses symbols and images intellectually.[99] Romantics lauded Mechthild as the poet and visionary mystically united with God. Romantics reacting to rationalism and the Enlightenment appealed to human feelings in religious experience. Their stress was on the aspects of personality that could not be reduced to powers of reason alone. The divine is holy, mysterious and incomprehensible. Hence they stressed a religion that looks inward and respects the role of intuition.[100] Certainly, Mechthild's epistemology is not restricted to knowing God by reason alone. She definitely uses reason, she communicates her spiritual message through the making of images. She saw herself making connection between God and humans through her words and she believed that the flowing divine love engulfs and unites the whole of creation.

---

[98] Caroline Walker Bynum, "Women Mystics in the Thirteenth Century: The Case of the Nuns of Helfta", in *Jesus as Mother: studies in the Spirituality of the High Middle Ages,* pp. 170-262, pp. 184-85, cited in Frank Tobin, *Mechthild von Magdeburg: A Medieval Mystic in Modern Eyes,* p. 123.

[99] Friedrich – Wilhelm Wentzlaff-Eggbert, *Deutsche Mystik zwischen Mittelalter und Neuzeit: Einheit und wandlung ihrer Erscheinungsformen,* (Berlin: de Gruyter, 1943, expanded ed. 1969), pp. 58-59 cited in Frank Tobin, *Mechthild von Magdeburg: A Medieval Mystic in Modern Eyes,* p. 55.

[100] Frank Tobin, *Mechthild von Magdeburg: A Medieval Mystic in Modern Eyes,* pp. 16-17.

Her intimate relationship with God, her visions, her passion, her participation in Christ's suffering, her deep sense of awareness of being one with God and of being separated and alienated from God – all inform her way of knowing God. And most significantly, one can easily discover that *eros* is the major theme underlying Mechthild's *The Flowing Light of the Divinity*.

Erotic Mysticism

As discussed earlier, Mechthild chooses to express her deepest experiences through courtly vocabulary and imagery. Spiritual experiences are expressed in erotic imagery. Mechthild draws from both scripture and secular imagery and courtly language is particularly pronounced in her writings. For Mechthild, the Song of Songs teaches the way of knowing God through the path of love. John Howard points out that the metaphor of the 'drunkeness of the soul' or the imagery of wine that Mechthild uses in her writings is found in the Old and New Testaments, especially in the Song of Songs.[101] Along with John Howard's thought, one may also observe that the themes such as love, desire, sorrow and fear that are found in Mechthild's book can easily find connections to the content of the book of the Song of Songs which served as one of the major resources for expressing Mechthild's own spiritual experiences. In her expressions, Mechthild makes God human by attributing to him qualities that would enable her to speak about erotic Divine love yet she does not lose sight of the real difference between human and divine. She moves from the sacral-feudal medieval mentality to courtly individualism. She gives importance to

---

[101] John Howard, "The German Mystic: Mechthild of Magdeburg", in *Medieval Women Writers,* ed. Katharina M. Wilson (Athens: University of Georgia Press, 1984), 153-85, pp. 158-59 cited in Frank Tobin, *Mechthild von Magdeburg: A Medieval Mystic in Modern Eyes,* p. 125.

individual experiences.[102] Mechthild by experiencing the love of the Beloved herself, turns biblical material into a historical note and thus offers a real love song.[103]

However, the connection between eroticism and religion is not exclusive to Mechthild but "pervades medieval literature since descriptions of the Heavenly Court often draw from contemporary society, and vice versa ..."[104] Erotic love as a way of speaking about the relationship between God and the soul became the most influential theme in the history of Christian spirituality, particularly in the medieval age. The Song of Songs is usually considered as offering a biblical grounding for erotic mysticism. In the early Christian writings, for example in Origen's writing, the soul is the bride and God the divine bridegroom. God embraces the soul, kisses her and wounds her with the wounds of his love.[105] For Origen, the knowledge of God was both affective and intellectual. It was sometimes described as *amor intellectus Dei*.[106] Illumination meant either intellectual cognition or an intimate relationship such as a couple knowing each other in sexual intercourse.

In the affective mysticism of the medieval age, the connection between eroticism and religion gained prominence. For instance, Bernard of Clairvaux speaks about kissing the Lord's feet, hands and mouth; the erotic imagery becomes the basis for his understanding of union with God. "The first kiss must be the penitent kissing the feet of Jesus, the second kiss must be the forgiven one kissing the hand of the Saviour, and

---

[102] See, Frank Tobin, *Mechthild von Magdeburg: A Medieval Mystic in Modern Eyes*, p. 66.

[103] *Ibid.*, p. 83.

[104] Susan Clark, "Introduction", *Flowing Light of Divinity*, p. xv.

[105] See, Grace M. Jantzen, *Power, Gender and Christian Mysticism*, p. 91.

[106] *Ibid.*, p. 93.

only then can one hope for 'a holier intimacy."[107] The three kisses correspond to the three stages of the mystical path namely, purgation, illumination and union. Thus the quest for union between the soul and the Lord is expressed in kiss in Bernard's writings.[108]

Mechthild's own usage of erotic imageries can be situated in the long tradition of erotic mysticism, yet, Mechthild shows her own independence and creativity which makes her erotic mysticism a type of its own. For example, in the courtly love poetry, the lady greets her lover. It is a gesture suggesting "conditional and restrained encouragement made by the lady to her lover and it is a promise of potential for the future." In Mechthild's writing, God greets the soul. The greeting gushes forth from the Trinity to the soul.[109] Thus, God promises the potential of a love relationship between the lady and Himself, which may possibly develop into a union between the two. However, Mechthild on her part also shows strong passion and desire to meet her Beloved, to be with him and to be united in love. In platonic understanding, the creature is restless until it finds repose in the unmoved mover of all love. In Balthasar's view, longing and desire dominate Mechthild's thought on union with God. Although, she uses courtly language, it is a "genuine rediscovery of Platonic eros."[110] He explains that "the

---

[107] *Ibid.*, p. 126.

[108] For more on Bernard's exposition of 'kiss' see, K. R. Sundarajan, "Bridal *Mysticism*, a Study of St. Bernard of Clairvaux and Nammālvar", *Journal of Ecumenical Studies*, 43, no.3 (2008), pp. 411-422.

[109] Frank Tobin, *Mechthild von Magdeburg: A Medieval Mystic in Modern Eyes*, p. 90, citing William Seaton, "Transforming of Convention in Mechthild of Magdeburg", *Mystics Quarterly*, 10, pp. 64-72, pp. 70-71.

[110] Hans Urs von Balthasar, "Mechthilds Kirchlicher Auftrag", in Margot Schmidt's translation of *Das fleißende Licht der Gottheit*, Dissertation, Freiburg University, 1955, p. 26, cited in Frank Tobin, *Mechthild von Magdeburg: A Medieval Mystic in Modern Eyes*, p. 62.

eros driving her to God is not some properly tempered human sentiment. It is something powerful, ruthlessly cruel, and it is so because for her it has its origin in God's own eternal nature."[111] Balthasar sees Mechthild experiencing God himself as the "ultimate restless lover burning with desire." He comments, referring to Book 2.24, "the world process, seen by antiquity as driven by eros, is subsumed by Mechthild into the Trinity: God the Father is the steward of this intoxicating life, the son is the chalice, the Spirit is the wine."[112]

This view seems plausible since in Book 2.24 Mechthild herself says in dialoguing with the apostle Paul which can be considered as one of her imaginative creative writing of her own inner impulses. It reads as follows:

> Paul, I was wondrously uplifted with you and have seen such a wonderful house that since then I have been able to be a living human being. When I think that there the heavenly Father is the innkeeper, and Jesus the cup, the Holy Spirit the pure wine, and the whole Trinity the filled cup, and love the mighty cellar, then God knows I would gladly accept if love were to invite me in.[113]

In Tobin's view, not all the descriptions of divine love in Mechthild's writings could be accommodated into a platonic mould. Tobin is right in saying this since it is discernible that the church fathers and medieval thinkers were well aware of platonic concepts, particularly the concept of *eros*, and more so they were imbued with this tradition of understanding of *eros*. No doubt, Mechthild might have been influenced by the platonic concept of *eros* yet not without a touch of her own

---

[111] Hans Urs von Balthasar, "Mechthilds Kirchlicher Auftrag", p. 32 cited in Frank Tobin, *Mechthild von Magdeburg: A Medieval Mystic in Modern Eyes*, p. 62.

[112] *Ibid.*

[113] Book 2. 24; Galvani, pp. 49-52, p. 50.

independence and creativity. For instance, *eros* that she experiences from God leads her to union as well as to a bitter and painful experience of abandonment. The fact that at times the soul feels deserted by God is explained by Mechthild as the freedom of God. God allows himself to be freely reached and also to be withdrawn. Only this freedom of God makes sense of the absence of God. At this point Balthasar seems right in saying that the absence of God is regarded positively by Mechthild since it is seen as the power to uplift the soul. In darkness and abandonment the soul understands not only that God is incomprehensible but also that even this "destruction of love must be a work of love" of the dearest companion.[114] Mechthild had a genuine love relationship with God, experienced Him as her Lord and Lover. This intimate love relationship was expressed intelligently in the contemporary erotic language that she was familiar with, grounding herself in scripture and finding vocabulary from the courtly love poetry. Her originality comes in the way in which she weaves them together. In Wolfgang Mohr's words, Mechthild's writing is "the boldest erotic poem that we have from the Middle Ages."[115] It is not too much to add that it is the boldest erotic poem of its own kind. In the next section we shall deal with her dialogical approach of presenting her love relationship with God.

---

[114] Hans Urs von Balthasar, "Mechthilds Kirchlicher Auftrag", p. 37, cited in Frank Tobin, *Mechthild von Magdeburg: A Medieval Mystic in Modern Eyes*, p. 62.

[115] Wolgang Mohr, "Darbietungsformen der Mystik bei Mechthild von Magdeburg", in *Märchen, Mythos, Dichtung: Festschrift zum 90, Geburtstag Friedrich von der Leyens*, Hugo Kuhn and Kurt Schier, eds., (Munich: Beck, 1963), pp. 375-99, p. 393, cited in Frank Tobin, *Mechthild von Magdeburg: A Medieval Mystic in Modern Eyes*, p. 83.

Woman's Way of Knowing: Dialogical

Mechthild tries to capture her experiences in words and presents them to her readers in a very admirable way. She presents her love relationship with God in dialogue form. Male and female; God and the soul speak, embrace, kiss and recognise each other's presence in the intensity of love. Elizabeth Petroff says that in the dialogues between God and the soul one can observe "an empowering and self-sacrificing love and an equally empowering yet sacrificial poverty or humility. Both voices express a love that is overpowering, both persons surrender to it, and both voices – God's and the woman's – characterize themselves with claims of humility or poverty."[116] The other feature of the dialogue between male and female is that both voices mutually enrich each other. Further, in dialogue, the two voices unite to form one voice as though they are inseparable yet there are still distinct.

It is similar to Mechthild's imagery of image and reflection. God and the soul are united like a mirror and its reflection. The soul becomes the image and God becomes the reflection. And God becomes the image and the soul becomes the reflection. This kind of oneness and duality is seen in other mystical writers too. For example, John of the Cross, speaking of his longing, and the drawing power of divine beauty, prays,

> that I may be so transformed in your beauty that we may be alike in beauty, and both behold ourselves in your beauty...hence, I shall see you in your beauty, and you shall see me in your beauty, and I shall see myself in you in your beauty, and you will see yourself in me in your beauty; that I may resemble you in your beauty, and you resemble me in your beauty, and my beauty be your beauty and your beauty

---

[116] Elizabeth Alvilda Petroff, *Medieval Women's Visionary Literature* (New York: Oxford University Press, 1986), p. 24, cited in Frank Tobin, *Mechthild von Magdeburg: A Medieval Mystic in Modern Eyes*, p. 104.

be my beauty; wherefore I shall be you in your beauty and you will be me in your beauty, because your very beauty will be my beauty; and therefore we shall behold each other in your beauty.[117]

Beholding each other, You in me and I in You are the ways of expressing knowing. It is non-dual yet the soul, or the I, is not absorbed by the Thou.

The knowledge of God is obtained through personal conversation between God and the soul. In the relationship between the partners the knowledge is obtained. In the knowing process the soul and God somehow become one yet do not lose their distinctiveness. Perhaps this is the knowledge of God that Mechthild experienced where knower and the known intertwine into a kind of non-duality that transcends all separation. Yet it is not a kind of oneness where distinctiveness is abrogated. Can this be called the self-knowledge of the soul? Ultimately, it is not self and knowledge but a self-knowledge of the soul which happens in the non-duality between the soul and God.

Walter Haug, analyzing the dialogue between the soul and God in Mechthild's writings, brings out another feature of the dialogue between the soul and God. He examines the whole process of writing down the experience of mystical union with God. In this process, the past is recapitulated and presented to form the possibilities of reactualizing the inexpressible experience in the readers. In this sense, it has a mission of forming the experiences of the mystic in the reader.

---

[117] John of the Cross, *The Collected Works,* translated by Kieran Kavanaugh and Otiolio Rodrigues, Washington, D. C.: Institute of Carmelite Studies, p. 547 cited in Grace M. Jantzen, *Power, Gender and Christian Mysticism,* p. 288.

He writes,

> It is unthinkable to write or even to speak when one is immediately one with God. The writing down of such an experience occurs of necessity at a distance. Insofar as the text thus reproduces a past experience, it is also a reaction to this experience; that is, it is, on the one hand, an attempt to come to terms with the incomprehensible while looking back on it; on the other hand, the distance to the experience has to become part of the subject matter. And this makes the portrayal of the union at the same time a portrayal of its loss. Thereby, however, by way of recapitulation of the mystical experience, the possibility of a new entering into the encounter reveals itself. And precisely here is where the call can go out to the potential reader: speaking has as its goal a reactualization of the mystical act; the text offers itself as a path to union; or, more precisely, the text takes as a theme the problem of how the portrayal of the experience remembered can function as a means of reactualizing the union.[118]

Haug's study shows that Mechthild re-creates her experiences through different temporal relationships. Her past and timeless experience of the Divine is presented in the present dialogue form. Hence the dialogue becomes an interplay between time and timelessness, between the particular and general. Tobin summarises Haug's study of Mechthild's dialogues stating that Mechthild "often allows the narrative framework to recede or disappear, so that one is left with pure dialogue to express the encounter between God and the soul. Since dialogue functions to re-create the present moment of the mystical experience, the predominance of dialogue gives immediacy to what

---

[118] Walter Haug, "Das Gerspräch mit dem unvergleichlichen Partner: Der mystisiche Dialog bei Mechthild von Magdeburg als Paradigma für eine personale Gesprächsstruktur", in *Poetik und Hermeneutik*, 11(1984), 251-79, p. 258, cited in Frank Tobin, *Mechthild von Magdeburg: A Medieval Mystic in Modern Eyes*, p. 92.

Mechthild writes."[119] The re-presentation or re-creation was a moment of giving birth in which we find an integration of Mechthild's own personality, her visionary experiences where she dialogues with the heavenly personage and the understanding that happens within. It is in reflecting, remembering and re-capturing that the past is made continuously present to the reader.

Dialogue implies a kind of duality or separation. There are two persons in dialogue. The theme of dialogue can be linked to the theme of alienation from God. In Haug's view, as Tobin puts it, embracing duality and separation is "the last possibility language can offer to help the mystic approach to God. By expressing separation and distance from God, language contributes by being a medium that does not mediate."[120] Haug states that "only a person who radically renounces everything that mediates has the opportunity of encountering the other immediately."[121] A mystic renouncing all that mediates can only resort to silence. This calls for an analysis of speech and silence.

Mystical Language: Speech and Silence

Mechthild's study on dialogue calls for an analysis of mystical language. The mystical experience cannot be captured by human words adequately. It must end in silence. According to Lüers, as Tobin explains, silence is "the most proper response to the basically inexpressible event of mystical experience

---

[119] Frank Tobin, *Mechthild von Magdeburg: A Medieval Mystic in Modern Eyes*, p. 94.

[120] *Ibid.*, p. 95.

[121] Walter Haug, "Das Gerspräch mit dem unvergleichlichen Partner: Der mystisiche Dialog bei Mechthild von Magdeburg als Paradigma für eine personale Gesprächsstruktur", p. 277, cited in Frank Tobin, *Mechthild von Magdeburg: A Medieval Mystic in Modern Eyes*, p. 95.

because silence is less material than language. Despite its lofty spiritual intent, mystical language can only be a secondary means of expressing of the divine."[122]

Susan Clark, analysing some of the medieval women's intense personal experiences with God, thinks that the experiences of these women show that the infinite for ever exceeds human words and articulations. They attempt to give a voice to what cannot be adequately expressed. Hence, one can observe a creative tension between "the desire to speak and the necessity to be silent."[123] Susan Clark says of Mechthild and other medieval women like Hildegard von Bingen, Margery Kempe and Julian of Norwich,

> Hildegard von Bingen's drawings and her divinely inspired admonishments and cosmology, Margery Kempe's uncontrolled weeping and peripatetic urges, Julian of Norwich's understanding of God as Mother, …These all speak to a need to approximate and disseminate intensely personal experiences that nevertheless have universal bearing. Mechthild von Magdeburg is a member of this particularly medieval community of mystics, and her only extant work well illustrates the strangeness and wonderment of revelation, the glimpses of Hell and Heaven, the fear and exultation, the disorientation and certainty, and the weakness and health that seem germane to the mystical experience. Clearly, something quite extraordinary happened – and continued to happen – to Mechthild von Magdeburg when she experienced her visions/dreams/revelations. As a subtext through her almost diaristic recalling of the experiences she underwent run fear, a sense of powerlessness and unworthiness, wonder at the splendours and horrors shown to her, as well as a frustration and an excitement at using

---

[122] Frank Tobin, *Mechthild von Magdeburg: A Medieval Mystic in Modern Eyes*, p.40, citing Grete Lüers, *Die Sprache der deutschen Mystik des Mittelalters im Werke der Mechthild von Magdeburg*, Munich: Ernst Reinhardt, 1926, p. 1.

[123] Susan Clark, "Introduction", *Flowing Light of Divinity*, p. xviii.

> language to approximate that which is beyond words, as she consorts with John the Baptist, Elias and Enoch, Christ, the Virgin Mary, Cherubim, and Seraphim. She searches for 'likeness', 'guises and disguises' and parables that can approach the truth indirectly, so that she frequently employs the Middle High German terms 'glich' ('like'), 'glichen' ('to resemble'), and 'gelichnisse' ('likenss' and, by extension, 'parable'), which not only attest to the difficulty of framing language but also to a desire to mask meaning from those who are not worthy of understanding it.[124]

Mystical experience struggles to express itself in rhetoric yet the mystic makes good use of language. But it is not conceptual language. It is emphatic language, in which unlike conceptual language, the word and object do not coincide but rather form an incongruence of word and object and thus leads towards a language which is in itself a "movement whose goal is immediate existential experience of God."[125] Hence, Tobin explains that for Haug, language has a lofty function to play. Language does not fail here but rather is used in a different manner without transcending the boundaries of language. Language can still be the medium by which the mystical experience is communicated. In Lüers's view, the mystics, although drawing upon the old religious imagery, present them in a new way. The imageries become fresh and acquires fresh interpretation because they come from direct inner experience. "Language is ennobled when used by the mystic."[126]

---

[124] *Ibid.*, pp. xviii – xix.

[125] Walter Haug, "Das Gerspräch mit dem unvergleichlichen Partner: Der mystisiche Dialog bei mechthild von Magdeburg als Paradigma für eine personale Gesprächsstruktur", pp. 270-71, cited in Frank Tobin, *Mechthild von Magdeburg: A Medieval Mystic in Modern Eyes*, pp. 94-95.

[126] Frank Tobin, *Mechthild von Magdeburg: A Medieval Mystic in Modern Eyes*, p. 40.

It is worth pondering Lüers's view a little more since as he thinks, Mechthild, by using courtly language, attempts to show the divine through these images. Thus, language becomes the medium of expressing the divine in fresh ways. If we examine Mechthild's writings in the light of Lüers's comments it becomes clear that Mechthild makes good use of language. For example, the way she expresses the idea of love is unique to her as a woman. Love is both a way of knowing and experiencing God and it is the instrument that links God with her. Love was bliss when she was united with her Beloved and it was agony and pain when she lost her Beloved and was alienated from him. Her love poetry was written in this joy and agony of meeting and parting and how a woman feels, longs and suffers come through in a unique way. Mechthild writes,

> Really pure love of God has four elements which never change. The first is growing desire, the second flowing torment, the third a burning sensation in body and soul, and the fourth is constant union combined with great caution. This state can only be attained when a complete exchange occurs with God, namely that you give God all that is yours, inwardly and outwardly, then will He truly give you what is His, inwardly and outwardly.[127]

Another example of Mechthild's use of language is in the way she gives a new interpretation of the image of light. In Mechthild's experience, divine love flows as light, perhaps not in accord with neoplatonic conception of love but Christologically "in the Incarnation as emptying of self."[128] Divine light flows down to the creatures as opposed to the

---

[127] Book 4.15; Galvani, pp. 112-113.

[128] Kurt Ruh, "Beguinenmystik: Hadewijch, Mechthild von Magdeburg, Marguerite Porete", *Zeitschrift für deutsches Altertum und deutsche Literatur*, 106 (1977), 265-77, pp. 273-74, cited in Frank Tobin, *Mechthild von Magdeburg: A Medieval Mystic in Modern Eyes*, pp. 73-74.

traditional image which portrays the soul striving upward to the light. God empties himself and flows down to the creatures.[129]

Like Light, the Holy Spirit, too, flows by nature into the valley. In a dialogue God speaks thus of the Holy Spirit:

> For the flood of My Holy Spirit
> Flows by nature into the valley.
> You find many a wise master, learned in the scripture
> Who himself is a fool in My eyes.
> And I will tell you more:
> It is a great honor for Me
> And strengthens Holy Christianity significantly
> That the unlearned mouth teaches
> The erudite tongues about My Holy Spirit.[130]

Holy Christianity is strengthened by the descent of the Holy Spirit in lowly and unexpected places and persons. The unwise and the unlearned teach the learned and the erudite. Thus, Mechthild is well qualified to teach and write. Her understanding of light and the Holy Spirit reveal a kenosis - fulfilment approach. For Mechthild, the Divine light flows and permeates all things. Divine reality is a creative flow of love and light. She calls her book the *The Flowing Light of the Divinity*. She presents a fluid nature of reality.

Also, in Book 2. 7 Mechthild brings yet another strand of thought using the image of light. She speaks of God appearing as a great light and offering two cups of wine, one filled with white wine of incomparable consolation and the other a cup of red wine of suffering. Both are given out of love and those who drink both are most blessed. There are two things to be

---

[129] Frank Tobin, *Mechthild von Magdeburg: A Medieval Mystic in Modern Eyes*, p. 67.
[130] Book 2.26; Galvani, pp. 56-57.

noted here: Mechthild's experience of God as a great light and the theme of light connected to both love and suffering. In Hans-Georg Kemper's view, this is an example of mixing symbols since the chalices represent "the chalice of consolation of the Last Supper and the chalice that caught the blood flowing from the side of the crucified Christ."[131]

This explains how Mechthild uses her mystical experience, the language that was available to her and her intelligence to convey her message to the readers. This is an exceptional contribution to theology from a woman mystic. She skilfully intertwines courtly language, the language in the Song of Songs and images available to her from her own context.

This kind of blending of two traditions, both the courtly love poetry and the mystical reading of Song of Songs in Beguine mystics, created a new genre of religious language which is termed *mystique courtoise* by Barbara Newmann.[132] Mechthild's skill and originality lie in using the contemporary love poetry in her own way, being open to God and ever eager to encounter new experiences with the bridegroom. Thus she is forever creating new knowledge for the benefit of her own spiritual growth and for edifying others. Ursula Peters comments that the medieval religious women show "a new openness to affective forms of expression for spiritual

---

[131] Hans-Georg Kemper, "Allegorische Allegorese: Zur Bildlichkeit und Struktur mystischer Literatur", in *Formen und Funktionen der Allegorie,* Symposium Wolfenbüttel, 1978, Ed. Walter Haug, (Germanistische Sympoien 3), Stuttgart, 1979, pp. 90-125, pp. 95-96, cited in Frank Tobin, *Mechthild von Magdeburg: A Medieval Mystic in Modern Eyes,* p. 84.

[132] Rosemary Radford Ruether, *Visionary Women: Three Medieval Mystics,* p. 34, referring to Barbara Newmann, *From Virile Woman to WomanChrist,* pp. 137-67.

experiences in association with the divine bridegroom."[133] This opens up an avenue for vernacular spirituality that is much more inclusive and welcoming.

In Morel's view, as Tobin states, the strengths of Mechthild are "the warm vitality in her descriptions of the feelings and moods of her heart, her vivid imagination, and her lyric talent." As to her weaknesses he mentions her "inability to stick to a logical plan of presentation and her failure to resist digressions in her narratives."[134] Morel's comments on Mechthild's imagination are worth pondering. Perhaps it can be stated that Mechthild had both visionary experiences and creative imagination. It can be called creative imagination since she had the ability to perceive and experience the vision to appropriate the vision and to re-create by way of re-presenting it in words, images and metaphors.

However, while it is right to say that Mechthild lacks a logical plan of presentation it is also worth considering the one single theme that runs through her writing. Mechthild's dialogues and narratives are based on the inherent theme of the relationship of the soul to God. This love relationship runs through her writing and ties it into a single comprehensive unit. Ruh's comment about Mechthild is refreshing. Ruh is captivated by Mechthild's way of presenting things. He calls her '*innocential spiritualis*' since "she expresses erotically daring things, but also blasphemy and theologically questionable things with a liberating candor.' Her use of language is artless, as though

---

[133] Ursula Peters, *Religiöse Erfahrung als literarisches Faktum: Zur Vorgeschichte und Genese frauenmystischer Texte des 13 und 14 Jahrhundrets*, p. 100, cited in Frank Tobin, *Mechthild von Magdeburg: A Medieval Mystic in Modern Eyes*, p. 128.

[134] Frank Tobin, *Mechthild von Magdeburg: A Medieval Mystic in Modern Eyes*, p. 37.

'inborn' or reflex, and it provides a look at religious subjectivity in the age of high scholasticism."[135]

A Mystical Text

Around 1345, a priest named Heinrich of Nördlingen sent Mechthild's text to a Dominican nun Margaret Ebner in the convent of Maria Medingen in Southern Germany. He thought that Mechthild's text evoked the same mystical experiences in him and hence it might do the same for the nuns at Maria Medingen. Heinrich commended this book to her to read saying that he was "compelled to do this by the living light of the fiery love of Christ. ..."[136] He further says, "Oh! I recommend to you all the treasure that God is in himself and has shown in this book."[137] Mechthild's text, probably along with the texts of other mystical women, was held as authoritative.

In the medieval age, one of the criteria for assessing the mystical authority of a text lay in its reproductive or generative power. Mechthild's text and probably those of other mystical women, was held as authoritative since it evoked mystical experiences in the audience. It connected the divine and human. It elicited the same divine love that it professed. For this reason such texts were considered as a sacrament or a sacred object. Text becomes "spiritual economies of exchange."[138] Text can

---

[135] Frank Tobin, *Mechthild von Magdeburg: A Medieval Mystic in Modern Eyes*, p. 74, citing Kurt Ruh, "Beguinenmystik: Hadewijch, Mechthild von Magdeburg, Marguerite Porete", p. 277.

[136] Patricia Zimmerman Beckman, "The Power of Books and the Practice of Mysticism in the Fourteenth century: Heinrich of Nördlingen and Margaret Ebner on Mechthild's Flowing Light of the Godhead", pp. 61-83, p. 62, citing *Letter* XLIII, Strauch, pp. 246-47.

[137] *Ibid.*,

[138] Patricia Zimmerman Beckman, "The Power of Books and the Practice of Mysticism in the Fourteenth century: Heinrich of Nördlingen and Margaret Ebner on Mechthild's Flowing Light of the Godhead", p. 78.

become a location of power since it is not merely a source of information but also a connector or creator of relationship between God and human, evoking mystical encounter with God. One meets the living presence of God in text. It serves as a catalyst in unleashing divine-human immediacy.

It also highlights the point at which the divine experience can incarnate in books. In the fourteenth century a circle of friends thrived on exchanging mystical treatises written by women. "Participation in such exchanges cut across the tidy, polarized lines historians often draw to describe society: noble/ lesser noble, religious/lay, male/female, Latin/vernacular, thought/experience. In essence, it cut across important markers and authority in medieval culture."[139]

---

[139] *Ibid.*, p. 83.

Conclusion

echthild focused on the interior dimension of the soul and emphasis is given to knowing God intimately. She appeals for feeling, passion, desire, longing, experience, reflection and imagination. Her longing love for God culminates in union. However, abandonment and alienation from God find centre place along with love and union in her spirituality. God reveals and conceals, is present and absent, gives pain and delight. God shows love and it is delightful. But for no apparent reason God seems to withdraw, hides and remains absent.

Mechthild's writings on abandonment by God make it clear that what is expected of religious men and women is not comfort but charity and obedience. The Union is lovely but it brings with it the mission of the lover which is to show charity and justice and to be a faithful representative of the lover on earth. We do not see in her life and teachings escapism, elitism, passivity, negation of self and privatism but rather a communitarian Beguine with an integrated spirituality aimed at transforming the world. Her loving relationship with the Beloved called for a disciplined and attentive regard for another.

She found repose in poverty, suffering, ill-health and the afflictions of love. She recognised human sin and wretchedness and divine greatness. However, there is place for corrections and the offer of the grace of God to help the soul. Her religion combines action and contemplation, knowledge and affection, understanding and love, knowing and doing. Love is the uniting link between the lover and the beloved. It is through the eyes of love the lover beholds the beloved. Hers is a Trinity-centred mysticism. The Trinity greets the soul in a loving embrace. This Trinitarian love transforms the way of knowing of God, speaking of God and understanding of self and society.

Mechthild's work reveals or tells much about the authority and performance of religious women in the medieval religion. The medieval religious women derived their self-confidence, religious authority and self-worth from their spiritual experience. Their teaching authority and leadership was democratic for it integrated public and private, religion and politics and reason and faith. The women's experience of the divine in dreams, visions and ecstasies gives a different methodology on the basis of different modes of experiencing and expressing the divine. Women's experiences cannot be ignored. The medieval religious women's experiences of visions, imaginative re-creations of Christ's passion and spiritual insight cannot be alien to biblical accounts of ecstasies, visions and dreams. Their experiences pave a new path to mysticism which gives space to women to articulate in new forms of language and modes of expressions.

In her text Mechthild herself negotiates with God and includes divine words among her words. In many places Mechthild attests divine authority to her text. Since it is divine-ordained, she, the unlearned, becomes the medium of communicating the message to all people. Hence, the dichotomy between learned-unlearned and clergy-laity is overcome in this understanding of power and authority.

Mechthild writes to all people, to a wider audience - both secular and religious. Her writing is a loving appeal to all. Her text lives on and the gift that she received from God passes on to others transcending all set boundaries like the Lady Wisdom who invites all to dine with her. It is worth concluding with the word of Heinrich of Nördlingen to the nun Margaret Ebner which might serve as an invitation to all men and women.

"O Margaretha, listen, daughter, and see, consider, and behold how sweet your lover Christ is. In Jesus Christ Amen."[1]

---

[1] "Patricia Zimmerman Beckman, "The Power of Books and the Practice of Mysticism in the Fourteenth century: Heinrich of Nördlingen and Margaret Ebner on Mechthild's Flowing Light of the Godhead", p. 62, citing *Letter* XLIII, Strauch, 246-47.

Bibliography

Allen, Charlotte, "The Holy Feminine", *First Things*, 98 (1999), 37-44.

Bailey, Michael D, "Religious Poverty, Mendicancy and Reform in the Late Middle Ages", *Church History*, 72, no. 3 (2003), 457-483.

Beckman, Patricia Zimmerman, "The Power of Books and the Practice of Mysticism in the Fourteenth Century: Heinrich Nördlingen and Margaret Ebner on Mechthild's Flowing Light of the Godhead", *Church History*, 76, no. 1 (2007), 61-83.

Brown, Colin, *Philosophy and the Christian Faith: A Historical Sketch from the Middle Ages to the Present Day* (London: Tyndale Press, 1969).

Bynum, Caroline Walker, *Holy Feast and Holy Fast: The Religious Significance of Food to Medieval Women*, (Berkeley: University of California Press, 1987).

Christ, Carol P., "Embodied, Embedded *Mysticism*, Affirming the Self and Others in a Radically Interdependent World", *Journal of Feminist Studies in Religion*, 24, no. 2 (2008), 159-167.

DeMayo, Thomas Benjamin, "Mechthild of Magdeburg's Mystical Eschatology", *Journal of Medieval History*, 25, no. 2 (1999), 87-95.

Fuller, Robert C., "Faith of the Flesh: Bodily Sources of Spirituality", *Religious Studies Review*, 33, no. 4 (2007), 285-290.

Gellman, Jerome, *Mystical Experience of God: A Philosophical Inquiry*, (England: Ashgate Publishing Limited, 2001).

Hollywood, Amy, "'Who Does She Think She Is?': Christian Women's Mysticism", *Theology Today*, 60 (2003), 5-15.

Hooper, Sarah, *Mothers, Mystics and Merrymakers* (Gloucestershire: Sutton Publishing Ltd., 2006).

Irigary, Luce, *Sexes and Genealogies* (New York and Chichester: Columbia University Press, 1993).

James, William, *The Varieties of Religious Experience*, The Gifford Lectures of 1901-2 (Glasgow: Collins, 1960).

Jantzen, Grace M, *Power, Gender and Christian Mysticism* (Cambridge: Cambridge University Press, 1995).

Jantzen, Grace M., *Becoming Divine: Towards a Feminist Philosophy of Religion* (Manchester: Manchester University Press, 1998).

Lerner, Robert E, "The Image of Mixed Liquids in Late Medieval Mystical Thought", *Church History*, 40, no.4 (1971), 397-411.

Magdeburg, Mechthild von, *The Flowing Light of Divinity*, translated by Christiane Mesch Galvani, edited with introduction by Susan Clark, Series B: Garland Library of Medieval Literature, 72 (New York & London: Garland Publishing, 1991).

McGinn, Bernard, "The Changing Shape of Late Medieval Mysticism", *Church History*, 65, no.2 (1996), 197-219.

McGinn, Bernard, *Foundations of Mysticism* (New York: Crossroad, 1991).

Moorman, John R. H, *Saint Francis of Assisi* (London: SPCK, 1963).

Peers, E. Allison, *Spanish Mysticism: A Preliminary Survey* (London: Methuen, 1924).

Petry, Ray C, ed., *Late Medieval Mysticism* (London: SCM, 1957).

Poor, Sarah S, "Mechthild von Magdeburg, Gender, and the 'Unlearned Tongue'", *Journal of Medieval and Early Modern Studies*, 31, no. 2 (2001), 213-250.

Poor, Sarah S, "Historicizing Canonicity: Tradition and the Invisible Talent of Mechthild von Magdeburg", *Women in German Year Book* 15 (2000), 49-72.

Poor, Sarah S, *Mechthild of Magdeburg and Her Book: Gender in the Making of Textual Authority* (Philadelphia: University of Pennsylvania Press, 2004).

Reuther, Rosemary Radford, *Visionary Women: Three Medieval Mystics* (Minneapolis: Fortress Press, 2002).

Roberts, Michelle Voss, "Flowing and Crossing: The Somatic Theologies of Mechthild and Lalleśwari", *Journal of the American Academy of Religion,* 76, no. 3 (2008), 638-663.

Schroeder, Roger SVD, "Women, Mission and the Early Franciscan Movement", *Missiology,* 28, no.4 (2000), 411-424.

Simons, Walter, *Cities of Ladies: Beguine Communities in the Medieval Low Countries, 1200- 1565* (Philadelphia: University of Pennsylvania Press, 2001).

Smith, Margaret, *Muslim Women Mystics: The Life and Work of Rabia and other Women Mystics in Islam* (Oxford: One world, 2001).

Solberg, Mary, *Compelling Knowledge: A Feminist Proposal for an Epistemology of the Cross* (Albany: State University of New York, 1997).

Sundarajan, K. R., "Bridal *Mysticism,* a Study of St. Bernard of Clairvaux and Nammālvar", *Journal of Ecumenical Studies,* 43, no. 3 (2008), 411-422.

Tobin, Frank, *Mechthild von Magdeburg: A Medieval Mystic in Modern Eyes* (Columbia: Camden House, 1995).

Underhill, Evelyn, *Mysticism: A Study in the Nature and Development of Man's Spiritual Consciousness* (London: Methuen, 1945).

Wiethaus, Ulrike, "Sexuality, Gender, and the Body in Late Medieval Women's Spirituality: Cases from Germany and Netherlands", *Journal of feminist studies in Religion,* 7, no.1 (1991), 35-52.

Wigner, Daniel E., "Clarity in the Midst of Confusion: Defining Mysticism", *Perspectives in Religious Studies*, 34, no. 3 (2007), 331-345.